MW01109653

Non-Payment in the Electricity Sector in Eastern Europe and the Former Soviet Union

Energy Sector Unit
Europe and Central Asia Region

The World Bank
Washington, D.C.

CONTENTS

The study was designed by Dominique Lallement and Gary Stuggins. Dr. V. Krishnaswamy carried out the study and wrote the report. Useful inputs and suggestions were provided by Nina Bubnova, Istvan Dobozi, Richard Hamilton, Laszlo Lovei, Tamas Markus, James Moose, Brian Pinto, Vladislav Vucetic, Jonathan Walters, Salman Zaheer and other Bank staff working in the region.

FOREWORD

This brief study reviews the non-payment problem in the electricity sector in Eastern Europe and the former Soviet Union during the period 1990-1997. It is essentially a desk study supplemented by a limited amount of field information provided by World Bank resident missions and consultants working in these countries. In addition to non-payment, the review also covers the problem of low cash collections and the preference in some countries for the use of cash substitutes such as barters, offsets, and promissory notes.

The non-payment problem is not confined to the electricity or the energy sector alone. It extends to a wide range of sectors in the economy. It emerged in the context of the major political and economic upheaval experienced by these countries in the early 1990s and its persistence and rapid growth, in turn, further aggravated the economic problems. Some of the countries managed to break out of the vicious circle and tamed the problem, while others are still struggling with it.

The objective of the study is to identify which policies and measures addressing the problem of non-payment in the electricity sector worked in practice and which did not. It includes, therefore, both success stories and failures. The study, however, is not intended to present a comprehensive analysis of the causes and nature of the non-payment problem. Rather, it is aimed at equipping Bank staff and decision makers with a set of practical tools that can be of use when the political will exists to tackle the problem.

Hossein Razavi
Director
Energy Sector Unit
Europe and Central Asia Region

ABSTRACT

This study presents the results of the research by a team of experts working in the energy sector of Eastern Europe and former Soviet Union. It is supplemented by eight brief country studies containing field data on the non-payment crisis in Albania, Bulgaria, Hungary, Armenia, Lithuania, Georgia, Russia and Kazakhstan.

The objective of the study is to identify successful policies and measures that were employed to address the problem of non-payments in the energy sector. Authors intend to present a wide range of data and practical suggestions that could be applied in different countries of the region.

PART I

MAIN REPORT

1. EXECUTIVE SUMMARY

A. Emergence of the Non-Payment Problem

1.1 Towards the end of 1980s, the centrally planned economic system collapsed in Eastern Europe and the Soviet Union and the ensuing transition of these countries towards market economy was characterized by the trauma of GDP collapse, run away inflation, rising unemployment and loss of traditional export markets as well as preferential trading arrangements. Traded energy prices quickly rose to international levels and the energy sector was hit with high supply costs, while the ability of consumers to pay declined sharply owing to loss of markets for the enterprises and declining income for households. The energy utilities thus accumulated huge arrears from their consumers and defaulted on their payments to their input suppliers, their taxes to governments, and the wages to their staff. In the former Soviet Union (FSU) states, insolvent enterprises started making payments with the products they manufacture (barter) or by cancellation of mutual debts (offset). Fanned by taxation based on cash receipts, and tax collection methods relying on routine freezing of bank accounts, resort to cash substitutes such as barter, offset, and promissory notes became widely prevalent leading to the practical disappearance of cash settlement from the energy sector.

1.2 Collections in Russia amounted to only 70% of the energy billed in 1996 and the share of the cash in total collections was only 16%. Collections in Armenia, Georgia and Ukraine were in the range of 57% to 86% and the share of cash in the collections was in the range of 20 to 60%. In Albania only 57% of the electricity generated was billed and of that only 53% was collected. In general the problem appeared to be strongly correlated to the depth and duration of the economic collapse. It was thus less severe in Eastern Europe and more severe in FSU states, the exceptions being Albania and the Baltic states. By and large countries dependent on energy imports seem to be adjusting somewhat faster than those with substantial domestic energy resources.

B. Impacts on the Economy

1.3 Poor collections and poorer cash collections quickly translated into a chain of inter-company arrears, bank arrears, tax arrears and wage arrears. Mounting tax arrears eroded the ability of the governments to provide adequate funds to the government budget entities (GBEs) to pay for their energy consumption, thus completing the vicious circle. Poor liquidity of the energy utilities led to maintenance backlogs, system deterioration, and lack of funds to buy fuel to operate the generating units. Thus in the midst of surplus capacity, these countries came to experience acute supply shortages, high supply costs and low system reliability. In Georgia and Armenia supply could not be maintained even for two hours of the day in most places including the capital cities. In Ukraine the concept of toll generation was practiced, whereby many units operated only when the consumer provided the fuel. In Russia poor liquidity caused irrational dispatch of inefficient units pushing up system variable costs significantly. The reliance on cash substitutes in Russia was driven by the desire to avoid tax payments and to make private profits at the expense of the firm. The volume of tax arrears there is seriously destabilizing the economy.

3

C. Causal Factors

1.4   The key factors which caused the emergence of the problem and its aggravation include:

- Tight monetary, income, and fiscal policies needed to control inflation led (in the initial stages) to payment defaults by: GBEs which could not secure adequate budget provisions; state owned enterprises (SOEs) and other enterprises, which had no access to budget support or bank financing, while they had lost their domestic and export markets; and households who were hit by declining incomes, rising unemployment and escalating energy prices.
- Inability of the utilities to disconnect supplies to non-paying customers, as governments maintained long lists of strategic consumers to which supplies could not be disconnected and zealous local politicians went on adding to this list a number of local industries to protect local jobs and local economy at the expense of the energy firms.
- Sheer lawlessness in Albania where consumers with guns stolen from the government threatened to shoot the utility officials, who attempted to disconnect defaulting customers.
- Technical inability to disconnect individual residential power consumers in countries such as Georgia, Armenia and inability to disconnect individual residential heat consumers in most countries.
- Dramatic changes in customer base with the share in total electricity consumption declining for industrial consumers (from 46%-57% range to 17%-50% range) and increasing for households (from 8%-25% range to 15%-52% range), making it more difficult to continue to cross-subsidize households by industries.
- Inability of the federal, regional and local governments to pay the mounting subsidies for households for power and heat to compensate the utilities for the tariff discounts they were compelled to offer by law to a wide range of households.
- Tax laws based on cash rather than on accruals and tax collection methods routinely relying on freezing bank accounts, which motivated the energy utilities in Russia, Ukraine and Georgia to minimize cash flow into their accounts and resort to the use of cash substitutes.
- The potential for private gain made the use of cash substitutes "popular" and extensive in these countries.
- Poor corporate governance arising from partial privatization of power utilities leading to the dominance of insiders in Russia and other FSU states.
- Federal-Regional tensions in Russia, and Central-Local tensions in Ukraine, where local officials tended to protect local jobs and local economy at the expense of energy utilities and prevented flow of cash from regions to the federal entities.
- Underdeveloped concepts of property rights and ineffective enforcement of such rights, combined with barriers to exit from investments through bankruptcy and liquidation.

D. Approaches to Solution

1.5   Part II of this report contains case studies relating to Albania, Bulgaria, Hungary, Armenia, Georgia, Lithuania and Russia and some notes on Kazakhstan. Based on these and the available information on Ukraine and Poland it is possible to identify practices at the utility level and the government level which help to mitigate the payment problem.

1. At the Utility Level

1.6   Practices at the utility level, which had helped to tackle the problem effectively include:

- Elimination of unmetered consumption, intermediate metering (such as apartment blocks and feeders), relocation of meters in locked boxes in places accessible to utility staff, meter testing, calibration and replacement-- the efficacy of these practices in preventing theft and improving collections has been demonstrated by the experience in Armenia, Albania and Georgia.
- Separation of meter reading function from the technical metering function on the one hand, and from the commercial functions of billing and collection on the other hand, has been shown to be effective in many countries in preventing collusion between staff and consumers.
- Computerization of consumer accounts enabling monitoring of each account and follow up for arrears through court systems and pursuing liquidation etc. had been shown to be effective in the East European countries and in the pilot areas in FSU states such as Russia, Georgia, Ukraine and Armenia.
- Insisting on consumers to pay their dues by check to the utility, or at the Bank or at well organized collection centers rather than paying cash to the utility staff reading the meter or serving the bill-- this has been shown to be effective in Armenia and Georgia to prevent leakage of revenue.
- Adoption of letter of credit based procedures to ensure timely payments from large consumers and escrow account procedures to ensure that the receipts of the distribution companies are fairly and quickly distributed to the transmission and generation entities and the fuel suppliers.
- Elimination of resellers and other intermediaries such as consumer associations enables better collection, and better cash collection by making disconnection of individual consumers for default possible.-- this is evident from the experience in several regions of Russia, Georgia and Armenia.
- Incentive schemes for the collection staff have to be designed carefully and properly, otherwise they could prove counterproductive, as was shown by the negative experience of Albania and Georgia. Poland appears to have positive experience, with the motto "My staff.. my most important customer"
- Making a list of top 25 to 30 consumers and monitoring their payment record by senior executives of the utility, who would also use their influence to help the customers to improve their cash flow has been shown to be effective by the experience in Bulgaria.

- Selling accounts receivable at reasonable discounts to banks and collection agencies seems to have proved a cost effective option in Hungary. Creation of a market for this could be a useful option.
- Combining heat and power distribution activities in one utility enables better collections from heat consumers, since power supply to them could be disconnected for default in heat payments. This was amply illustrated by the experience of Tractebel S.A., in Almatyenergo of Kazakhstan and in Lithuania, when the Lithuanian Power Company (LPC) handled both operations. But this option may not be replicable everywhere.
- Price discounts to improve cash collection is being tried in Russia; the results are yet to be evaluated. This double edged weapon, like tax amnesty, has to be used very carefully and for limited periods only.
- Use of prepaid meters for power could be good option to improve collection from households. The results of the experiment going on in Telasi area of Georgia are yet to be evaluated.

2. At the Government Level

1.7 Practices at the government level which have been found to be effective in mitigating or eliminating the problem include:

- A broader focus on the fiscal deficit , during the stabilization phase, enabling a greater congruence between macro and micro policies and ensuring that fiscal deficit targets are met *after* settling, in full, all dues payable for government consumption and purchases to SOEs (especially to the energy entities) and not by accumulating arrears to such entities to avoid capital consumption in those sectors. This was amply illustrated by the positive experience of Bulgaria, Hungary, Poland and Lithuania and the negative experience in other FSU states.
- The degree of substance and effectiveness of the legal infrastructure, property rights and systems to enforce property rights (including the right of the energy supplier to deny supplies to those who do not pay for it), unhampered entry and exit policies for investments and orderly and speedy procedures for bankruptcy and liquidation. This accounts for the relative success of the Central and Eastern European states and relative lack of success in FSU states.
- Adoption of stern and effective ways of dealing with GBEs such as: agreeing in advance with them on their level of energy consumption, providing adequate earmarked and non- fungible line item provisions in the budget for payment of such agreed consumption, monitoring their payment performance and taking disciplinary action against the heads of offices who exceed the agreed level of consumption, fail to pay the dues or divert funds for other purposes and also exposing them to the discipline of disconnection of

supplies for non-payment[1]. The effectiveness of such an approach was amply illustrated by the experience of Lithuania.

- In respect of SOEs providing such services as drinking water supply, sewerage etc. adopting tariffs which generate adequate revenues **at least** to pay for the operation and maintenance (O&M) costs, which include the cost of power supply.

- Adjusting tariffs in a timely fashion to cost recovery levels (and to approach marginal supply costs) and to eliminate internal cross subsidies, enables utilities to improve quality of supply and thereby improve collections. This was illustrated by the experience of Bulgaria and Hungary. The nexus between quality of supply and collections was amply illustrated by the experiences in Georgia and Armenia.

- Replacing arbitrary and unsustainable price discounts to a wide range of households (to be compensated by subsidy payments to the utilities by the governments), by targeted means-tested subsidy to the poorer families paid directly to them as a part of the social security payments encourages better collection from the households. Experience in Hungary, Armenia and Bulgaria (energy vouchers) amply illustrate the efficacy of such social safety net strategy.

- Creating too many small sized distribution enterprises to decentralize power distribution to the municipal levels should be avoided, as such enterprises lack economies of scale and good corporate governance. Georgia and Armenia are reversing such decentralization based on negative experience. Georgia, Albania and Armenia are consolidating their distribution enterprises to achieve economies of scale and to privatize them.

- Sector unbundling and privatization could generally help, but only if good corporate governance could be achieved and strong mechanisms to enforce contracts[2] and competent and independent regulation are in place. In the absence of these, unbundling and half-hearted privatization could actually aggravate the problem as can be seen from the experience of Russia, Armenia, Albania and Georgia. Experience in Hungary, Bulgaria and Poland shows that payment problem can be solved through good corporate governance even when the utility is state owned or vertically integrated.

- Orderly corporatization, commercialization and privatization to strategic investors help as can be seen from the example of Hungary.

---

[1] In Lithuania, the exception to this were only such institutions as fire service, biological research labs etc. But even the heads of departments of such institutions were liable for disciplinary action for diversion of funds for other purposes.

[2] These could include letter of credit arrangements and escrow account arrangements among the members of supply chain and with major consumers to ensure fair and quick flow of cash to all members of the supply chain. Effective dispute resolution methods, such as binding arbitration should also be in place.

E. Lessons for the Bank

1.8   As a result of this brief review of the payment problem in some of the East European and FSU countries, a few key points emerge as possible lessons to the Bank in its operation in these countries. They include:

- In view of the close linkages between the non-payment problem and the macroeconomic issues in these countries there is a need to focus on such cross cutting aspects as *corruption* and *governance* and these are best handled by modes of lending such as a combination of : (a) Structural Adjustment Loans (SALs) and Sector Adjustment Loans (SECALs), and (b) carefully targeted investment lending as well as carefully designed Economic and Sector work (ESW) . Extensive work with the utilities in the field would be needed to improve the systems and procedures, staffing and training and the Bank may have to mobilize substantial grant funds and work closely with bilateral donors to ensure well coordinated ESW and institutional support work.

- The coordination of adjustment lending with IMF programs should result in the broadening of the focus on fiscal deficits to ensure that fiscal deficit targets are attained only after the government fully discharging its payables to the energy utilities for its consumption, and in the inclusion of conditionalities relating to energy sector, such as collection performance (especially collection of dues from GBEs), cost recovery and social safety nets.

- While energy sector ESW and lending should focus on the non-payment problem, loss reduction and theft, one should not lose sight of the perennial concerns of sector viability (cost recovery, external subsidies, internal cross subsidies) and consumer interests (least cost operation and supply, social safety nets, quality of supply and environmental mitigation). Good tariffs and good collections must go together. Often non-payment problem disappears when sector viability and quality of supply improve.

- There is no single ideal sequence of reform applicable to all countries. The sequence among stages of reform such as sector unbundling, corporatization, commercialization and privatization should be decided on a country specific basis depending on its circumstances.

- Approach to sector restructuring and unbundling should be cautious and should take into account the paramount need to create simultaneously competent and independent sector regulation and strong enforcement mechanisms to ensure contract compliance. In their absence, unbundling may actually aggravate, *inter alia*, the non-payment problem.

- The key to solving the non-payment problem is good corporate governance. Evidence exists that good arms length corporate governance leads, *inter alia*, to better collection performance even when the utility is state owned and vertically integrated. (see examples of Hungary, Poland, Bulgaria etc.)

- Where such good arms length corporate governance fails to develop, unbundling and privatization may have to be accelerated.

- Clear evidence exists that privatization to strategic investors yields the best results (from the point of view of securing good corporate governance needed to solve the non-payment problem) and that it is advantageous to privatize distribution utilities first.
- Bank's operations need to focus on the federal, regional and municipal inter-relationships, devolution of responsibilities, authority and resources and through ESW should seek to improve them. Sector structures should be designed to be in consonance with such political realities, rather than causing permanent strains.

2. THE NON-PAYMENT PROBLEM

A. Emergence

2.1   Towards the end of 1980s, the centrally planned economic systems collapsed in East Europe and Soviet Union leading to major political and economic turmoil. The Soviet Union split into Russian Federation and several independent countries and were collectively referred to as former Soviet Union (FSU) countries. In the process of their transition to democracy in politics and markets in economics, the East European and FSU countries experienced in the early 1990s, a traumatic contraction in GDP, runaway inflation, a sharp drop in domestic demand, a steep rise in unemployment and huge fiscal deficits. The dismantling of the Council of Mutual Economic Assistance (CMEA) led to: (a) the disappearance of the hitherto sheltered export markets and preferential pricing and trading arrangements; (b) the devaluation of their currencies by orders of magnitude; and (c) huge current account deficits. Table 1 attempts to present the depth of the macroeconomic changes in select countries belonging to this group.

2.2   The impact of this turmoil was specially harsh on the energy sector of these countries. Traded fuel prices quickly rose to international levels and became available only against the payment in hard currencies. The sector was hit by high prices of inputs and a lack of hard currency to pay for them at a time when demand, as a function of contracting GDP, contracted even more rapidly. Falling incomes and the urgently needed macroeconomic stabilization measures sharply reduced the ability of energy consumers to pay for their consumption, leading to a huge non-payment problem in most of these countries. While the problem was faced by all sectors in the economy, it was most acute in the network service utilities such as those of electricity, district heating and natural gas, because of the difficulties (social, political and practical) in disconnecting supplies to defaulting consumers.

Table 1: Macroeconomic Changes in Select East European and FSU Countries.

Country (Currency)	Real GDP Contraction 1990 GDP index = 100			Average Annual Inflation (%) 1990-1996	Range of Fiscal Deficit as a % of GDP		Fall in Nominal Exchange Rate Relative to US Dollar		M2 as a % of GDP	
	Period	Cumulative drop (%)	1996 GDP Index		Period	Range	Period	Local currency to one $	Period	Range
Albania (Lek)	1990-92	40	85	68.5	1990-95	31-10	1990-96	10 - 107	1990-96	33-69
Bulgaria (Leva)	1990-93	27	67	158	1992-96	5.2-13.4	1992-96	7 - 496	1991-96	46-65
Hungary (Forint)	1990-93	18	86	24	1991-96	8.2-2.2	1990-96	62 - 165	1991-96	42-51
Poland (Zloty)	1990-92	18	104	35	1991-96	6.7-2.8	1990-96	0.95-2.9	1991-96	32-38
Lithuania (Litai)	1990-93	61	42	298	1990-96	0.8-5.4	1993-96	3.9-4.0	1993-96	22-14
Armenia (Dram)	1990-93	69	37	2364	1991-96	56-1.8	1993-96	75 - 443	1993-96	90 - 8
Georgia (Lari)	1990-94	72	31	2556	1991-96	26 - 3	1993-96	0.1 -1.28	1992-96	31-4.5
Kazakhstan (Tenge)	1990-95	43	57	1090	1990-96	7.9 -1.3	1992-96	0.8-73.3	1992-96	45- 4.4
Russia (Ruble)	1990-96	43	57	646	1992-96	21.6-5.5	1990-97	2-5939	1993-96	19-3.1
Ukraine (Karbovenet)	1990-96	61	39	2278	1992-96	25.4-3.2	1992-95	242-158302	1993-96	32-1.6

Source: Country Assistance Strategy Reports of the World Bank and Transition Report 1997 of EBRD.

Note: Ukraine currency was changed to Hryvnia in 1996. $1 = Hr 1.88

B. Dimensions

2.3   The non-payment problem has two other dimensions. First, the energy utilities facing acute shortages of revenues, in turn defaulted on their payments to their input suppliers, their banks, and in their tax payment to the government, further straining the government's ability to fund fully its own energy consumption and thus creating a vicious circle. Second, in the absence of domestic and export markets for their products, the insolvent industrial enterprises, especially in the FSU countries, started paying their dues with their products (barter) or by promissory notes (vexels). Energy companies started settling their dues among themselves and with their suppliers, by mutual or cyclic cancellation of their debts. This process is referred to as offset or set off[3]. Thus even when payments were made, they were mostly by way of barter, vexel or by offset, leading to a rapid decline in the share of cash transactions. Thus in FSU countries-- especially in Russia, Ukraine, Georgia, and Armenia -- the non-payment problem was characterized by an increase in non-cash transactions, inter-company debts and large tax arrears of the energy entities.

2.4   Thus in Russia at the level of the 72 AO Energos[4], collections as a percentage of billings in the power and heat sectors was estimated to be only 70 % in 1996, while the share of cash in collections was only 16%, the rest being in the form of barter, vexels and offset. During January-August 1998 collections reached 84% of billings and the share of cash in collection improved marginally to 17.6%. Consumers' total debt to all 72 AO Energos was estimated at 123.5 billion rubles ($20 billion). At the end of August 1998, the accounts receivable of RAO UES-the federal holding company of the power and heat companies, doing wholesale business amounted to 12.2 billion rubles ($2 billion) or about 13.5 months' sales. The situation relating to the other countries is summarized in Table 2.

2.5   It may been seen from Table 2 that the non-payment problem has largely been overcome in the East European countries, while it continues to be a serious one in FSU countries. The exceptions to this statement are Albania and Lithuania. Albania in the former group is unable to collect because of the widespread violence and criminality in the country, while Lithuania of the second group has achieved a degree of success through stern and disciplined remedial action. Also countries endowed with plenty of domestic energy resources among the FSU states (such as Russia, Ukraine and Kazakhstan), continue to have serious problems[5], while countries which are import dependent for their energy resources (such as Lithuania and Armenia) seem to have made or be seen to be making some headway. Collection from households is the key problem in Albania, Georgia, and Armenia, while collection from industrial enterprises and GBEs is the problem in Russia, and Ukraine. Use of cash substitutes is the key problem in Russia, Ukraine, Georgia, Armenia and Kazakhstan.

---

[3] The words "offset" and "set off" are used interchangeably in this report.

[4] Regional utilities supplying electricity and heat.

[5] Albania, with hydro power resources adequate to meet its power demand, also falls into this category.

Table 2: Dimensions of the Collection Problem in Select ECA Countries

Country	Year	Collection (as a % of billings)	Cash (as a % of collections)	Remarks	Key Problem Areas
Albania	1997	58	97	end 97 A/R= 11 months sales	High level of system losses and theft of power; low collections. Largest share of arrears are from SOEs (49%) and households (40%).
Bulgaria	1992	75	100	end 92 A/R =3.04 months sales	Collections from SOEs used to be a problem
	1997	91	100	end 97 A/R = 36 days sales	Payment problems have largely been overcome.
Hungary	1992	85	100	end 92 A/R=1.79 months sales	Collection from SOEs and household heat consumers is used to be a problem.
	1997	96	100	end 97 A/R=14 days sales at the level of MVM Rt., the grid company	Payment problems in respect of power have largely been overcome
Poland	1994	90	100	end 93 A/R =36 days sales at the level of grid company.	Collection from SOEs and heat supply networks and municipal entities used to be a problem
Lithuania	1993	87	100	end 93 A/R= 47 days power sales	Largest arrears were from Government and municipal budget entities (50%) followed by those from households (35%) and agricultural consumers(15%).
	1993	70	100	end 93 A/R =110 days of heat sales	
	1997	96	100	end 97 A/R = 13 days sales for power	Collection problem largely solved.
	1997	91	100	end 97 A/R = 34 days heat sales	
Armenia	1992-95	30	25	Data at the level of distribution companies	Low collections; low cash collection; persistence of offsets as a form of payment. Households with a share of 50% in sales account for 55% of non-payment; and Drinking water companies, agriculture and irrigation with a share of 13.2% in sales account for 23% of the non-payments.
	1996	65	60		
	1997	62	64		

Country	Year	Cash collection	A/R		Comments
Georgia	1996	57	..		Low level of collections; low level of cash collections. Persistence of barter and offsets as forms of payment. Collections of distribution companies are not passed on to others in supply chain. Households with a share of 57% in sales account for almost 100% of non-payment.
	1997	70	37	Grid company level[6]	
	1997	68	36	Distribution co. level	
Kazakhstan	1997	93	33	Data for 10 distribution companies with KEGOC (grid company)	Payment by barter, offsets etc., is the key problem. Also distribution companies do not pass on collections to others in the supply chain.
	1997	72	..	Data for KEGOC	
Ukraine	1994	83	..	Data for Grid Co.	Low levels of collection and very low levels of cash collections. Persistence of barter, offsets and promissory notes as forms of payment.
	1996	86	20	Data for Energos	
	1997	91	18	Data for Energos	
Russia	1996	70	16	Data at the level of AO Energos	Low level of collections and very low levels of cash payments; persistence of payment by barter, offset and promissory notes; high degree of leakage of revenues. Resellers and distribution companies do not pass on collections to others in the supply chain. Largest shares of arrears are from Industry (36.5%) Federal, regional and local budget entities (25%) and resellers (22%)
	1998	84	17.6	January-August 1998	

Source: WB Internal Documents

Note: A/R denotes accounts receivable.

[6] There is reason to believe that percentage of cash collection may have been overstated in the case of Georgia.

2.6   A comparison of the data in Table 1 with the results in Table 2, indicates the close correlation between the depth and duration of the economic debacle and the persistence of the non-payment problem. In the East European states, GDP started recovering after three years of decline, and   inflation was substantially lower and was brought under control, more quickly than in the FSU states. The range of fiscal deficits, currency devaluation, and money supply constraints were also much less onerous than in FSU states. Thus East European states showed a greater ability to adjust to the trauma of transition than the FSU states. The FSU states are still suffering from lack of growth, a fragile situation regarding inflation, and the need to maintain tight monetary and fiscal policies. The results in their fight against the non-payment problem follow this grouping closely. Albania with reasonable economic performance and Lithuania with moderate economic performance are the exceptions to this generalization, the former because of its problem in controlling violence and criminality, and the latter because of the exceptional level of discipline and maturity shown in managing its crisis.

C. Impacts

2.7   The consequences of such a high level of non-payments had been enormous both at micro and macroeconomic levels. The poor collection at the distribution companies translates into their arrears to the transmission and generating companies, which in turn accumulate arrears with their suppliers and contractors. The power companies build up arrears with gas companies and coal companies and gas companies build up arrears with their foreign suppliers often resulting in supply disruptions. Most companies default on their tax payments to the government, often default on their dues to the banks and accumulate wage arrears to their employees.

2.8   In Georgia, the inability to pay for the imported fuel and war damages to the hydro facilities resulted in a serious shortage of power supply which had to be rationed till mid 1995 with daily supplies not exceeding a few hours even in the capital city. Power supply in Armenia was reduced merely to two hours per day in 1993, since Armgas, the gas utility could not settle its debt to Turkmenistan for gas purchases. As of April 1997, the Armenian energy sector debts to Turkmenistan and Russian fuel suppliers amounted to $98.15 million and its debts to domestic suppliers, contractors and the government amounted to $ 55.57 million. The energy sector debts thus exceeded 10 percent of the country's GDP. In Russia, 19 energos (out of the total 72) for which data was available, had tax arrears exceeding $ 790 million towards the end of 1997. Tax dues from Gazprom and other energy sector entities in Russia have reached significant dimensions, while the government's arrears to them were believed to be even greater. This vicious circle was causing a major macro economic problem in the country.

2.9   In Russia, many of the more efficient large thermal power plants owned by RAO UES are unable to operate for want of cash to purchase fuel, resulting in the system dispatching power from the smaller and inefficient units owned by the regional power companies, which being in the retail business have a better cash position than RAO UES. Also fuel purchases by the thermal units through the use of barter and vexels results in much higher prices being paid for them, than would otherwise be the case. The needless incremental variable costs incurred in the system have been estimated by the Energy Research Institute in 1996 to be of the order of $ 3.0 billion or 20% of the total variable costs. Reports by Mc Kinsey seem to indicate that such incremental costs may even be substantially higher. In Ukraine, Georgia, Kazakhstan and Armenia, the situation was similar. For want of cash, the utilities had to postpone or forgo the planned maintenance, rehabilitation and reinforcement of their systems, resulting in poor heat rates, high system losses, frequent supply interruptions and near total loss of system reliability. They face ironically severe power shortages in the midst of falling demand and excess capacity. In Ukraine thermal power plants were operated, whenever the buyer provided fuel -- a phenomenon known as "toll generation".

2.10 The plant load factors (PLF) in FSU states as a whole dropped from 61% in 1990 to 50% in 1994. The drop in the PLF of some of the FSU states is summarized in Table 3 below. The steep drop in capacity utilization is attributable not only to the decline in demand and the splitting of the united energy system of Soviet Union, but also substantially to the inability of the generating companies to operate their units for want of funds needed for fuel, O&M, rehabilitation and wages.

Table 3: Capacity Utilization in the Power Sector of FSU

Country	Capacity (GW)	Utilization % 1990	Utilization % 1994
Russia	205.6	60.1	46.9
Ukraine	54.3	62.8	42.8
Kazakhstan	16.9	59.0	46.7
Lithuania	5.1	63.6	31.8
Georgia	5.1	32.7	14.8
Armenia	3.8	31.2	17.1

Source: WB Internal Documents

2.11 In countries such as Lithuania, Hungary and Bulgaria, the arrears of energy companies threatened the stability of the banking system, as energy arrears quickly translated into banking arrears, because of the phenomenon of "soft banking". In most countries, the build up of inter-company arrears, arrears to the banking system and tax arrears seriously eroded the discipline needed to enforce the tight fiscal and monetary policies required to achieve macroeconomic stability. In Russia, and to a slightly lesser extent , in other FSU states, the problem is a continuing one.

2.12 The extensive resort to non-cash settlement of dues in Russia, Ukraine and other FSU states distorts the market through their opacity and high transaction costs. The ambiguity in valuing non-cash transactions leads to a lack of trust in the balance sheets of the companies and to a transfer of resources from the efficient to the inefficient segments of the economy. It enables tax evasion and is effectively used as a mechanism for minimizing the flow of funds to the federal government and federal agencies, thus creating serious economic problems.

3. CAUSAL FACTORS

A. Effects of Stabilization Measures

3.1   Essentially, the non-payment problem arose and assumed serious proportions in the context of the economic collapse. The measures taken to stabilize the economies also tended to aggravate the problem in the short run. The intensity of the problem varied as a function of the depth and duration of the economic collapse and the severity of the remedial measures called for. Macroeconomic programs attempting to rapidly lower inflation by stabilizing the exchange rate through high real interest rates could contribute to payment arrears and non-cash settlements. This is especially the case when fiscal policies are not correspondingly tightened and reliance on debt issues to finance fiscal deficits is high; the manufacturing sector gets crowded out of the credit market as funds flow to the treasury bills. Weak expenditure control, likewise, leads to delays or arrears in payments for energy services directly contributing to non-payments. Thus in the early phases of stabilization:

- flow of funds from the budget to bail out state owned energy enterprises was cut off;
- government budgets provided inadequate funds to government budget financed entities (GBEs) (such as departments and agencies, hospitals, schools, courts etc.) to pay for energy consumption on the same scale as before. GBEs tended to divert these funds for more pressing needs in the context of poor budget controls, resulting in the accumulation of arrears from the *GBE segment*;
- the industrial enterprises were deprived of budget support and bank loans at a time when they had lost both the domestic and export markets. They started defaulting on their payments to utilities, banks and the government resulting in the accumulation of arrears from the *industrial segment*; and,
- declining incomes, high inflation, high unemployment and steeply rising prices of power and heat (in local currency terms) severely eroded the ability of households to pay for the level of energy consumption to which they were used to. This resulted in an accumulation of arrears from the *households segment*.

B. Inability to Disconnect Supplies for Non-Payment

3.2   In the context of accumulating arrears from households, GBEs, and industries, the key aggravating feature was the significantly weakened existence of the standard remedy available to all utilities in the world, namely, the ability to reduce or disconnect supplies of power or heat to the non-paying customers. In the FSU states, especially in Russia, Ukraine and Georgia, the traditional legal concepts relating to the provision of heat and power supply appeared to stand in the way of the utility trying to disconnect supplies for non-payment. RAO UES[7] notes in its key reform document (1998) that "there is collision

---

[7] The national level power company in Russia which operates the nationwide transmission system and owns substantial generating capacity (See Russian Case Study in Part 2).

17

between the public nature of power supply agreement under the civil code of Russia and the enforcement of user payment." Despite the enactment of new Energy Laws in many FSU states, the conflict between the old and new laws existed enabling confused court systems (not used to concepts of market economy) to hinder successful disconnection for non-payment. There have been instances of courts ruling that "electricity not being a commodity or a physical article, could not be stolen".

3.3 In most FSU countries, the governments maintained a key list of strategic customers to which power and heat supplies could not be cut despite continued default in payments. Through sheer abuse of political power and influence, and in their short sighted anxiety to protect "local jobs and the local economy", politicians at the federal and regional levels kept on adding to the strategic list all kinds of insolvent industrial establishments and often even solvent ones. On top of these constraints, the utilities themselves were not keen to 'kill the goose' and cut off supplies to industrial consumers and lose the market from major consuming segments.

3.4 In Albania people threatened to shoot the utility officials who attempted to disconnect defaulting customers. In Georgia and Armenia absence of adequate metering, and the location of the meters inside the apartments effectively prevented any action against theft of power and non-payment. Technical conditions in the dilapidated network did not facilitate the orderly disconnection of non-payers, without affecting the paying customers as well. In most FSU and East European countries technical designs of the heat supply network did not enable households to reduce heat consumption even if they wanted to; nor did it permit the disconnection of supply to individual consumers. In any case disconnection of heat supply to households in northern Europe during winter is never an easy option. Finally disconnection of supplies to hospitals, fire services, drinking water supply agencies, army and the police is not a viable, or practical, option for obvious reasons.

C. Unsustainable Subsidies

3.5 The earlier approach to tariffs for power and heat supply in these countries involving production subsidies to energy entities and consumption subsidies to consumers could not be sustained in the wake of steep rise in the price of fuels and in the context of the imperative need to cut down fiscal deficits. Production subsidies represented government bail out of energy companies, for having failed or delayed to set "cost recovery tariffs". Consumption subsidies for heat supply were provided as a function of the household income, the size of the apartment and the number of persons living there. Consumption subsidies for power supply were meant to subsidize the consumption of power by a wide range of "privileged consumers" such as war veterans, Chernobyl victims, earthquake victims, militia, retirees and pensioners, policemen, judges, employees of the city government, blood donors, handicapped persons etc. Many categories get a 50% discount and some get a 100% discount. In Telasi distribution company of Georgia for example, 13% and 4% of the residential consumers get 50% and 100% discounts respectively. The subsidies to such consumers amounted to about 4% of the annual revenues in 1997. For Georgia as a whole, the government was obliged to pay $ 2.34 million per month as subsidy for power consumers in 1997, approximately 0.5 %

of the country's GDP. In Mosenergo of Russia, 33% of the total heat revenues in 1996, came by way of a subsidy from the Moscow municipality for keeping the tariff for residential consumers low. In Lithuania, the annual heat subsidy in 1997 to consumers amounted to $50 million or about 0.5 % of the GDP. Subsidy payments in Ukraine for energy consumption by households amounted to over 5% of the total government expenditure in 1992. The subsidy system operated by the FSU governments involved large expenditures from the budget, but were inefficient and unsustainable. In Hungary, subsidies for heat and power were estimated at 13% of the GDP in 1989, but were brought down to the level of about 4% by 1993. In most FSU countries (Lithuania is an exception) the governments were unable to make adequate provisions in the budget for these subsidies. Also when the subsidies were routed through the budgets of regional or municipal governments, they tended to be "hijacked" by these governments for other needs. The non-receipt of such massive subsidies from the governments was a major component of the non-payment problem. Even when the budgets provided for subsidies, as in Georgia, they were never disbursed; they were only adjusted or set off against the tax dues from the utility.

3.6   Traditionally the power and heat tariffs for households in these countries were maintained at levels below the cost of supply and that for industrial consumers was kept substantially above the cost of supply thus allowing industries (economic consumption) to cross subsidize households (social consumption). During the days of central planning, the share of industries in total consumption was so high and that of household so low, that this kind of cross subsidy could be tolerated to some extent. With the collapse of the centrally planned economic system, the share of industrial consumption declined and that of household increased making this cross subsidy mechanism unsustainable. Table 4 below attempts to summarize the change in the relative shares of these two categories of consumers in these countries.

Table 4: Changes in the Power Consumption Mix

Country	Year	Share of Households (%)	Share of Industries (%)	Year	Share of Households (%)	Share of Industries (%)
Albania	1990	9.1	48.9	1994	42.4	29.2
Bulgaria	1988	25.2	56.5	1996	37.9	50.4
Hungary	1984	23.0	50.0	1995	33.8	40.0
Poland	1985	14.0	57.0	1995	17.5	48.0
Lithuania	1990	12.0	54.0	1995	23.0	42.0
Armenia	1985	16.0	50.0	1997	50.0	17.0
Georgia	1989	17.0	46.0	1997	51.5	20.7
Russia	1990	11.0	57.0	1996	29.0	51.0
Ukraine	1990	7.9	54.4	1995	14.2	42.7

Source: WB Internal Documents

In countries like Albania, Armenia and Georgia, the significant increase in the share of the households and their inability and or unwillingness to pay for their consumption is the key cause of the non-payment problem. The combination of internal cross subsidies, subsidy for privileged consumption and tolerance of non-payment is believed to have led to excessive and wasteful specific consumption in the household sector. Instances of use of electric cooking ovens for apartment heating have been recorded.

D. Tax Laws and Their Enforcement

3.7   The cash strapped energy companies started the practice of cancellation of mutual debts first with their suppliers and later with governments (their tax dues against subsidy and GBE dues from the government). The energy companies in FSU states also accepted barter payments from industrial enterprises, which had no cash to pay. This, in turn, let loose a long chain of barter to enable the goods to reach the ultimate users. Promissory notes or vexels came in handy, eliminating the clumsy transportation and storage involved in barters. In Russia, Ukraine and Georgia, these non cash transactions flourished and dominated collection because of the nature of the tax laws and the manner of their enforcement. Value added tax as well as the corporate profit tax were based on cash accounting (and not on the basis of accruals), thereby providing an incentive to accept only a minimum of cash and collect the balance by way of non-cash transactions. Also in Russia, the tax authorities routinely froze bank accounts of energy companies for tax arrears and any money credited into those accounts went straight to the treasury and not the companies. Thus the key motivation for the widespread pursuit of non-cash transactions is tax payment avoidance, as well as tax minimization. Further, in the absence of suitable and effective oversight for promissory notes and similar instruments, their valuation is suspect, providing scope for managers and employees of energy companies to personally profit from their use. Thus even when consumers (such as households) paid their dues in cash, utilities in Russia, Ukraine and Georgia devised elaborate methods to ensure that cash did not flow into their accounts converting cash payments into non-cash forms through third parties. Thus, cash collection levels in Russia and Ukraine tended to stagnate at around 10% to 15%, just enough to pay the wages.

E. Poor Corporate Governance

3.8   The corporate governance of the energy entities in FSU states (with the exception of Lithuania) was poor both when they were state owned and when they were "privatized" using mass privatization methods of allocating shares to the employees and managers. Financial controls were weak and internal audit and credible external audit were practically non-existent and accounting standards fell far short of IAS. The share holding in the privatized utilities (especially in Russia) was such that there were no dominant shareholders to provide effective corporate governance. The environment was conducive to the utility executives making private profit through non-cash transactions and enjoying power, patronage, comfort and benefits, clearly not possible under a cash regime.

F. Federal- Local Tensions

3.9   In federated states, like Russia, the interference from regional and local officials prevents the flow of cash from the regional energo to federal government and federal agencies.. The local officials tend to harass the utility officials, who show any inclination to disconnect non paying industries. They are also known to compel the utilities to procure all their requirements from local industries, regardless of the quality or price. Similar behavior on the part of local officials have been reported in Ukraine and Georgia.

G. Concept of Property Rights

3.10 Finally, the existence of the concept of property rights and institutions such as independent courts and impartial arbitration panels to enforce them or to resolve disputes vary greatly among these countries. Similarly the efficacy of the liquidation and bankruptcy proceedings against defaulting insolvent companies to protect the interests of creditors, as well as the social and political stance towards exit by way of bankruptcy vary widely among these countries. Thus East European countries such as Hungary, Poland and Bulgaria and among the FSU states, Lithuania, have more advanced systems in this regard, and have been able to overcome the problem of arrears. The remaining FSU states have mechanisms not yet adequately effective to enable utilities to move successfully for the liquidation of their insolvent customers.

4. APPROACHES TO THE SOLUTION

4.1   Case studies relating to Albania, Bulgaria, Hungary, Armenia, Lithuania, Georgia and Russia are given in Section II of this study. These case studies attempt to outline how the countries have tackled or are tackling the problem and to what extent they have succeeded. Based on these case studies and the information available on Ukraine, Kazakhstan and Poland, this chapter outlines possible approaches to the solution both at the utility level and at the government level.

A. Approaches at the Utility Level

(i) Metering

4.2   At the level of the utility a number of key steps have been shown to be necessary and effective in the battle against power theft and non-payment. Provision of meters to all customers (especially those living in apartments in high rise buildings), meters for the apartment building as a whole including the common service areas therein, meters for the feeders and at the substations have been found necessary in Armenia, Albania and Georgia to track the accuracy of consumption and loss by way of theft. The Armenian experience clearly demonstrated the importance of relocating the meters in locked boxes in the ground floor or the basement of the apartment buildings for easy access by utility staff and for preventing tampering by customers. The Armenian example also highlighted that customers themselves would be willing to bear the cost of relocation (with the utility providing the locked boxes), as long as supply reliability could be restored. This aspect could be relevant for replication in all countries in which theft of power by the households and collection from households are the key problems. Albania has already sought the Bank assistance for adopting these methods. Apart from installing meters at all strategic points, they should (following the standard operating procedures of modern utilities) be read and analyzed at set intervals, tested, calibrated and replaced periodically.

(ii)   Organization of the Commercial Functions

4.3   The next key step relates to the organization of the functions of meter reading, billing and collection, customer accounting and follow up (see Box 1 on Good Utility Practices on Consumer Receivable). Technical departments of the distribution network should handle the responsibility of installing customer meters, checking their accuracy, calibrating them and replacing them when necessary. The meter reading function must be carefully separated from these technical groups as well as the commercial groups in charge of billing and collection, to avoid collusion and to enable greater control. Computerization of customer accounts and instituting suitable control over staff and flow of cash have been shown to be necessary nearly in all countries. Experience in Armenia and Georgia highlight the need to avoid the practice of residential consumers paying their bills in cash to the utility staff who come to read the meters or present the bill. Consumers should be encouraged to mail their checks to the utility, or pay in cash in the banks or in the properly staffed collection centers of the utility (with appropriate cash control mechanisms). Residential consumers almost always pay in cash and do not use non-cash mechanisms. It is therefore necessary to design fool proof methods and systems to ensure that 100% of the payments reach the account of the utility.

Box 1

Good Utility Practices on Consumer Receivable.

- At the time of giving connection to any new consumer, the utility should collect not only the capital cost of service drops, wiring and meters as consumer contribution, but also a deposit equal to the estimated consumption of the customer for two or three months, depending on the meter reading and billing cycle (usually once in one or two months) adopted by the utility.
- The value of the consumer deposit must be periodically updated to match the increasing consumption levels. Such updating must be at least once in two or three years. The consumer deposits should be retained in accounts earning market rates of interest.
- If billing is based on consumer reading his own meters, ensure monitoring of consumer consumption record, as well as physical check by utility staff at least once a year, if not more.
- Organize computerized consumer accounts in which the consumption levels and payment performance of each consumer over time could be fully and continuously tracked and monitor accounts which show deviant behavior.
- The consumer bills should indicate the normal amount to pay if paid within the period of 2 or 3 weeks allowed for payment and the penalty for late payment, say within 4 to 8 weeks.
- Reminders should be issued routinely once in two weeks after the first 3 weeks, incorporating a notice informing the customer that service will be cut off if payment is not received within the allowed period. When payment is not received till the end of the period for payment with penalty, a formal notice indicating the date and time for disconnection of the service should be issued to the consumer.
- Unless payment has been received by then, disconnection must be carried out as scheduled. Where violence against disconnection is suspected (as is often the case in Albania) management should arrange for the police protection of the utility staff in advance, or organize utility's own security staff.
- Reconnection may be effected only upon payment of all arrears and payment of reconnection charges and revised consumer deposits, if need be.
- The accounts receivable should be "aged" and collection of outstanding debt should be pursued even after disconnection, through collection agents, or through court cases coupled with vigorous enforcement of court decisions. A small and effective legal team should be set up to handle such cases.
- Examine carefully the cost-effectiveness of selling such consumer debts at a suitable discount to banks or other institutions willing to buy it (Hungarian example).
- Write off hard core irrecoverable debts.
- Follow consistently the accounting policy of making provisions for bad debts and doubtful debts in accordance with IAS.
- In the case of large industrial and commercial consumers, who may have significant monthly variations in cash flow, negotiate a rescheduling of payments based on interest rates slightly higher than market rates.
- In the case of large insolvent customers, join hands with all creditors (especially banks) and work on a plan to restructure and reschedule debts, and when that fails, move for the liquidation of the company.
- In the case of budget financed entities, assist the federal, regional and local governments to decide on realistic consumption levels for these entities at the time of budget formulation, keep track of the line item provisions in the budget and alert the government of any suspected diversion of the funds. Present the government at least once a month a list of delinquent entities with details of arrears in a form which the government can easily understand and follow up.

(iii) Elimination of Intermediaries

4.4   Outsourcing the meter reading, billing and collection functions have been practiced widely in all these countries through the institution of "resellers". Most of the regional energy companies in Russia (Energos) have their own Energosbyts, a division performing these functions[8]. Still resellers are used in a wide range of areas. By and large the institution of resellers had been a major source of indiscipline in Russia, Georgia, Armenia and Ukraine. Normally they are expected to collect the full tariff, retain their commission of 8 to 10%, and remit the balance to the account of the utility. Most resellers collect the dues, but do not pass on the share of the utility fully or punctually, thus placing the utility in an awkward situation, since the utility can not disconnect supplies to consumers (and penalize the paying customers) on the ground that resellers did not remit the collections to its account. In most of these countries, the collection performance of the reseller segment is the worst. In the Telasi area of Georgia, collection from resellers was at 15% while the average collection was over 60%. Based on such poor performance the resellers are being phased out in Georgia. In many regions of Russia (such as Komi, and Novosibirisk), the experience had been similar and the resellers are being phased out. In Komi region of Russia, the services of all resellers have been phased out by the end of 1998. The key reform document of RAO UES (1998) clearly recommends the elimination of resellers as an important component of reforms needed to improve collection performance.

4.5   Use of consumer cooperatives as a vehicle for collection is similar in character to the use of resellers and experience in Armenia (where it was tried during the period of acute supply shortages, when the non-payment problem was the worst in the household sector) showed that it was subject to similar infirmities within a few months. Some of the members did not pay, and in some cases, the office bearers embezzled the collections and the utility could not penalize the consumers, who had paid the dues to the office bearers. By and large, technical functions in power distribution as well as the commercial functions (such as meter reading, billing and collection) are best done by the utility directly dealing with the consumers, avoiding all kinds of intermediaries.

4.6   In Telasi region of Georgia, a distribution system based on the use of pre-paid meters is in experimental operation covering 1500 consumers. Electronic pre-payment meters have been installed by Energia, a Georgian- Israeli Company which buys power from the local power distribution company at the rate of US cents 2.45/kwh and sells power to consumers at the price of US cents 3.4/kwh set by the National Electricity Regulatory Commission. Energia guarantees collections and payments to the distribution company. The results of this experiment are yet to be evaluated. In areas where a significant portion of the total sales goes to a large number of consumers each with a very small level of consumption and where acute collection problems from households

---

[8] Though Energosbyts are divisions of Energos and have no separate legal personality of their own, they are treated as if they have such a status and their accounts are not subject to freezing by tax authorities for the tax arrears of Energos. This needs further examination and review.

exist, pre-payment meters could be a cost effective solution. It may be worth examining whether it could be used in Armenia and Albania.

(iv) Incentive mechanisms for Utility Staff

4.7   Albania's experiment in providing for its utility managers and staff, salary supplements for better collections and salary reductions for poor performance did not prove successful and had to be withdrawn, since courts held that utility staff and managers could not be penalized for customers' default! This suggests that incentive schemes should be carefully designed as a supplement to the base salary. The compensation structure should consist of a competitive base pay for normal performance standards and a significant level of incentive pay, which will vary as a function of the level of superior performance. Service conditions and contracts must provide for due process for reduction of base pay or dismissal for performance below normal standards. More importantly the staff must be motivated to contribute to the design of the incentive system, target determination and the role each has to play using techniques similar to Management By Objectives (MBO). The experience of Polish distribution companies in "treating their employees as their most important customer" is an excellent example of how to motivate the staff for high levels of performance and loyalty to the company, in the context of major changes in the business environment. Assistance for design and implementation of an appropriate incentive system in the utilities based on successful experience in the West could be an important contribution from the Bank in these countries.

(v) Heat Consumers

4.8   Technical designs of district heating systems in these countries makes it difficult to disconnect heat supply to individual apartments for payment default. Disconnection of *power supplies* for default in payment for *heat* has been used with success in Lithuania, when LPC was in charge of both heat and power supplies. After the decentralization of heat distribution to municipalities in 1997, this option was no longer available. In Kazakhstan, Tractebel S.A., was able to acquire both the power supply and heat supply franchises for the Almaty area, and was able to use this technique quite effectively to reduce heat arrears dramatically. It is doubtful whether such a combination could be effected in every country or even in all regions of Kazakhstan. However, a privately owned heat distribution company (AES Silk Road) in another part of Kazakhstan came up with an imaginative solution to the problem by disconnecting heat supply to the entire apartment blocks with many defaulting households while protecting the interests of paying households therein, by giving them free electric space heaters and paying the cost of their incremental power consumption. Heat supply was restored to the building only after the defaulting households settled their bills. With the cooperation of local authorities, it should be possible to replicate this experience in other countries. In the long term the key area for reform in the heat sector seems to be to improve the design of district heating systems to enable consumers to adjust the level of their consumption (in response to price signals) and to enable the utility to disconnect supply for defaulting customers, or to change over to a more decentralized system of providing individual heating system for each house or building.

(vi) Working with Large Consumers

4.9 It is absolutely necessary that disconnection must be available as a credible threat in respect of large industrial and commercial consumers, and the energy supply company must have the freedom to disconnect for non-payment. But this by itself is not sufficient. As was done in Bulgaria, a list of the top large industrial and commercial consumers accounting for a substantial percentage of total sales should be compiled and each of them carefully monitored by senior executives of the power utility, to understand the nature of the business of the customer and its pattern of changes in cash flow and develop payment schedules to match them[9]. The Bulgarian utility looked upon such customers as key business partners and was willing to use its influence, credit rating and contacts to secure new export or domestic sales contracts for these businesses to improve their cash flow, thereby improving its own collections. This kind of a partnership approach could have relevance in many of the FSU states.

(vii) Price Discounts to Consumers

4.10 To improve cash collections, non-price incentives of uninterrupted supplies, guaranteed supplies etc., have been offered in some countries. The results of such initiatives are inconclusive at best. Armenia offered at the height of its power scarcity preferential supplies to those who were willing to pay in advance. Georgia offered guaranteed supplies to those who settled their bills regularly, and Ukraine offered toll generation to those who paid for the fuel or provided fuel for the generating units. These can only be regarded as reasonable "fire fighting solutions". In the context of scarcity, when loads have to be shed, one could conceive of shedding the loads from those who habitually default, provided system conditions would permit such selective shedding. In the earlier years RAO UES of Russia had offered 30 to 40% price discounts for cash payments and did not meet with any significant success. It has been conjectured by observers that the profit in the use of cash substitutes was perhaps much higher than the level of these cash discounts. In the second half of 1998, the President of Russia issued a decree enabling the power companies to give 50% of the power price as discount, in a move to liquidate arrears and to improve cash collections. Data is not yet available to evaluate fully the efficacy of this move. However, there is reason to believe that the habitual non-payers who enjoyed a "100% discount" would not find the 50% discount attractive, while customers who were paying regularly at the full price became eligible to pay with a 50% discount! Russia is also operating a New Energy Market run by a non-profit organization "Independent Financial Operator", in which only the consumers who are willing pay in cash and pay in advance, and only the generators who are willing to

---

[9] Examples would be flat monthly payments, equal monthly billing arrangements etc.

give the prescribed cash discount are allowed to participate[10]. In the last year or so, the membership of this arrangement seemed to be growing[11]. It is difficult to take a view on the soundness of such initiatives. The practice is somewhat akin to the concept of tax amnesties, which have been criticized as rewarding tax evasion and encouraging tax defaults in the long run. Price incentive schemes may have the pernicious effect of perpetuating tariffs at non-viable levels, especially when the present price levels are barely adequate to meet often understated costs of supply. Such discounting and preferential treatment practices should only be used as temporary measures and should not be a part of any long term solution. Russian attempts to improve cash collections should rather focus on corporate governance(to identify and discipline misbehaving managers who make private profit through non-cash transactions), better oversight of vexels and elimination of barters, introduction of IAS and external audits and, more importantly, on reform of tax policies and tax collection methods, as well as privatization of AO Energos to strategic investors, which are discussed in the next section.

B. Approaches at the Government Level

(i) Broader Focus for Stabilization

4.11 At the government level there should be a clear appreciation of the linkages between macroeconomic policy (fiscal, monetary, trade, exchange rate, incomes and wages) and microeconomic policy (sector structure, ownership, competition, entity survival and viability, entry and exit). A more comprehensive approach to fiscal deficits, covering not only the government budget deficits, but also the deficits of government owned utilities, enterprises and banks would introduce greater discipline and lead to more effective stabilization. Often the narrow focus on the government budget deficits alone (on a cash basis and ignoring its huge payables to energy entities) has led, in most of these countries, to tolerance of mounting utility arrears, using them as a cushion to protect the people from the immediate effects of stabilization. The relative success in Lithuania, Bulgaria, and Poland is explicable in terms of a better understanding of these macro-micro linkages and a willingness to tackle the deficit at all four levels. The success of Hungary was also initially based on a similar approach , later greatly enhanced by effective privatization of banks and enterprises to strategic investors. In the other FSU countries, stabilization programs, in the earlier years, tended to focus mostly on government budget deficits resulting in the tolerance of growing arrears in the energy, enterprises and banking sectors, often resulting in the arrears of the government owned utilities and enterprises being covered by soft financing by government owned banks.

4.12 Sequencing and timing of the stages of reform are also the key to the success. Stabilization of the economy comes first, and in this stage, strains will be felt in the energy sector. It should be quickly followed by the second stage of restoring the viability

---

[10] The perception is that prices in the regular wholesale market are high as they cover the high transaction costs of a range of barters and vexels, while the prices in the NEM could be lower since such financing costs are not applicable in a cash based market.

[11] The most recent information indicates that this operation is likely to be merged with the regular wholesale market operations of FOREM.

of the energy entities in preparation for the final stage of their meaningful and effective privatization to cut their umbilical chord to the government financial system. In FSU states, especially in Russia, the first stage of stabilization is still going on and ineffective mass privatization (except in parts of Kazakhstan) has preceded utility commercialization and viability, creating new and unhealthy vested interests militating against economic efficiency.

(ii) Legal Framework and Exit Policies and Practices

4.13 Governments have to legislate for a clear and unambiguous recognition of various kinds of property rights (including the right to own the land on which the fixed assets are built), as well as for the speedy registration, trading, transfer and enforcement of such rights at reasonable costs. The legal systems must enable resolution of property disputes through arbitration or through independent court systems at reasonable costs. The legal systems must also enable the enforcement of contractual rights and liabilities. In many FSU states (especially in Russia and Ukraine), despite the passing of new laws, courts have difficulty in regarding heat or electricity as capable of being stolen and in recognizing the utilities' right to refuse supplies to defaulting customers. The success in

---

Box 2

Set Off Mechanism

1.   Extensive resort to the mechanism of set off is one of the reasons for the liquidity crunch experienced by the energy utilities in the ECA region. In the simplest case it involves only two parties. For example the payable of the power company for the purchase of fuel could be set off against the receivable of the power company from the fuel company for consumption of power. Set off can take place in a triangular fashion when the tax arrears of a power utility are set off against the stock of past power consumption arrears of government entities financed from the state budget. Often tax arrears of energy entities are set off against consumer subsidy payments due from the government for providing power at subsidized rates to a wide range of consumers.

2.   While an occasional use of such set off is perhaps harmless, systematic and frequent use of it can and does result in inefficiencies and distortions. The routine use of set off to clear the current dues and past arrears of government budget entities, fosters budget indiscipline. The budget entities may no longer make an attempt to estimate correctly their energy needs, and may not care to limit their consumption to the budgeted levels. Further more they may routinely divert for other purposes the provisions in their budget for energy payments. Thus set off should only be used in exceptional cases, preceded by a reprimand of the defaulting budget entity and by its assurances that in future it would live within its budget.

3.   In Russia, Ukraine and other FSU countries, set off often involves several parties in the payment chain rendering the transactions opaque and difficult to audit. The government of Armenia, for example, has formally prohibited such chain offsets and tolerates only the one-on-one kind with proper recording and verifiable valuation. Further in the context of high inflation in these countries (often in 3 digits), it is doubtful whether the items set off had been valued properly, taking into account the time value of money. In the end, for practical reasons, companies are better off in collecting their dues and paying their bills in time than by resorting to set off in which they stand to lose interest charges unless all the related transactions have taken place at the same time and unless the cost of money is same for both parties.

4.   Finally, as has been pointed out in the case of barter and promissory notes, the widespread use of offsets, encourages irresponsible consumption (on both sides of the transaction), which would not normally be possible under a cash regime.

Lithuania, Bulgaria, Hungary and Poland can largely be attributed to the progress made in the building up of the legal infrastructure suitable for transition to a market economy.

4.14 Arrears from state owned industrial enterprises is the most significant component of the non-payment problem. The key to the success in tackling this is the governments' exit policy for the industries sector. Insolvent enterprises should not be allowed to drain the resources of the economy. The exit policies should incorporate elements such as: (a) isolation of insolvent enterprises in a "Chapter 11" like environment to protect the interests of all creditors and to give a chance to the enterprise to move back to normalcy in agreed time frame; (b) restructuring the debts to enable such recovery and to protect the interests of all creditors; (c) restructuring the enterprise and selling it or other privatize it in a time frame agreed with creditors; and (d) quick and efficient liquidation and bankruptcy procedures, when efforts to sell the enterprise fails. Such an exit policy should be complemented by initiatives to retrain displaced workers and to provide new job opportunities, by following unhindered entry policies for investment. Such an approach should also be in conjunction with banking reform, forcing the banks to conform to the prescribed capital adequacy ratio, minimize their infected or non-performing portfolio and work with other creditors in placing the insolvent clients in isolation and later, when warranted, move for their liquidation. Hungary and Bulgaria seem to have done a relatively better job in this area, resulting in their ability to nip the problem of non-payment in the bud. Reforms in FSU states (except in Lithuania or in parts of Kazakhstan) in this regard are not adequate, explaining to a large extent the continuation of the non-payment problem.

(iii) Approach to Non-cash Settlements

4.15 Governments in FSU states need to make major efforts to discourage non-cash settlements of government debts, tax debts and energy debts. While straight forward mutual cancellation of bilateral debts is not by itself pernicious, triangular offsets and multiple chain offsets create problems of ambiguity in valuation, promote inefficiency and lead to a loss of budget control (see Box 2 on Set-off mechanisms). Armenia's example of formally prohibiting multiple and chain offset is noteworthy, but it does not seem to have succeeded in eliminating such transactions (perhaps because the government itself has not given up its practice of setting off its subsidy debts and energy debts to the utilities against the tax debts of utilities to the government). On the basis of conditionalities agreed with the Bank and IMF, the federal government of Russia has issued decrees prohibiting offset as a mechanism for payment of federal taxes. This has not prevented the regional and municipal governments from receiving their taxes through offset. In Russia and Ukraine (and perhaps Georgia too), the key area for reform is the rationalization of taxes and tax collection methods. First, taxation must be based on accruals (with adequate provision for writing off bad debts) and not on cash receipts and expenses. Once this is done, part of the bias against cash receipt will disappear. Second, the practice of routine (and almost perpetual) freezing of the bank accounts of firms defaulting in tax payment, which is not conducive to promote cash collection, should be changed. Such freezing must be selective, limited to short duration, and imposed only upon the basis of court order for recovery. Third, the corporate tax must be on the basis of profits calculated on the basis of using IAS, and after fully allowing for the proper valuation of offset, barter and vexel based transactions. The adoption of GAAP and IAS, and independent external audit of all corporate entities are necessary to impart transparency and credibility to financial statements and to have better control over the valuation of non-cash transactions. Fourth, Central Banks should explore the possibility of creating an oversight mechanism for the issuance, valuation and secondary trading of promissory notes (vexels) and similar instruments covering both cash vexels and commodity vexels (see Box 3 on Barter and Promissory Notes).

(iv) Approach to Government Budget Entities

4.16 In respect of energy dues from Government Budget Entities (GBEs), the deduction at source from the budget and direct transfer to the utilities could only be an interim measure and not a regular solution (see Box on Good Practices in Relation to Budget Entities). Budgetary procedures and budget controls must be substantially upgraded as was done in Lithuania. Reasonable levels of consumption of power and heat must be agreed upon with each head of department, and adequate, earmarked, non-transferable and non-fungible funds should be provided as a line item in the budget of the department. The budget should be carefully monitored through the year, and heads of departments who misappropriate these funds for other purposes must be disciplined with serious punishments. Once this mechanism is introduced, then the utilities must be given the freedom to disconnect the GBEs for payment default. Lithuania achieved excellent success in this regard, and its practice could be replicated in other countries. Armenia, Bulgaria, Hungary and Poland have also made good efforts in this regard. In respect of agencies such as drinking water supply companies (i.e., those providing basic needs and collecting revenues), tariffs for water must cover in full at least the O&M expenses (which include the cost of power for pumping) to ensure that water companies are able to pay their energy bills.

Box 3

Barter and Promissory Notes (Vexels)

1. In the context of tight fiscal and monetary policies pursued in FSU countries, enterprises attempted to maintain their production and employment levels by resorting to the practice of barter. At the beginning of the collapse of the economies, enterprises simply continued to deliver to each other, hoping for a state bail-out. When it became clear that there could be no state bail out, they resorted to bilateral barter of their products. However, since suppliers could not always directly use the goods received in payment, they had to sell them or arrange for another barter in exchange for their own needed inputs. Thus one barter led to another, leading often to a long chain of multiple barters, before the products reached the end user. Debts, taxes and to a lesser degree wages and company benefits came to be settled by barter. The share of barter deals in the total industrial sales in Russia is estimated to have risen from 17% in 1994 to 47% by the end of 1997. Such a steep rise in barter transactions appears to be strongly correlated with the rise in the level of inter-enterprise arrears, wage arrears and tax arrears.

2. Barter occurs not only among producers, but also between producers and state budgets. The largest percentage of barters (55%) relates to the sale of intermediate goods such as fuel and electricity. Since power and heat suppliers in the FSU states (especially in Russia and Ukraine) were not free to cut off supplies to non-paying enterprises, they accepted barter as something better than nothing. However, barter transactions lack transparency, involve considerable under or over valuation of the goods, and often lead to a significant level of under-the-table type payments and profits. The value of goods in barter deals could be 30 to 50% higher than their cash purchase value. This enabled many utility managers to skim-off the profits from barter transactions through an intermediary to handle all such transactions. The intermediary collects cash from the customers, then uses this cash to purchase the goods and inputs needed by the utility and transfers them to the utility at barter prices inflated by 30 to 50%. The rapid increase in barter transactions has been attributed mainly to: (a) the wide spread practice of the tax authorities in routinely freezing the bank accounts of utilities for tax arrears to ensure that any cash going into them could automatically be transferred to the treasury for tax arrears; and (b) the weak corporate governance structures of even the "privatized" utilities, enabling utility managers to divert company profits to personal gain through the use of intermediaries for handling barter transactions.

3. Promissory notes (or "vexels" as they are called in Russia and Ukraine) are securities which entitle the owner the right to claim certain property of the debtor (issuer). Under conditions of tight money supply and high interest rates, vexels came into vogue as money substitutes. Quickly they became convenient instruments to facilitate multiple barter transactions, avoiding the cumbersome need for storage and transport of goods. Typically the power grid company issues a vexel to the power generating company in exchange for the purchased power. The latter endorses the vexel to the construction company for construction services. The construction company endorses the vexel to the power distribution company for receiving power supply. The power distribution company exchanges the vexel with the power grid company for power received, thus completing a cycle of non-cash transactions. There could be very many variations in the transactions and the cycle could in fact be very much larger involving a wide range of companies. The energy companies handle these transactions through an intermediary-- usually a lending company-- and minimize the flow of cash into the their accounts, lest it be seized by tax authorities. Vexels are discounted based on the financial strength and the liquidity position of the issuer and the valuation agreed upon in each transaction is not transparent and is not subject to any regulatory oversight. This provides scope for considerable personal/ private gain through the use of intermediaries.

4. According to an OECD survey covering 26 regions in Russia, vexels are used by regional and local governments extensively as they accounted for 50% of their revenues and 39% of their expenditures. They are used to cancel out long chains of arrears. Like barters they are a mechanism to avoid payment of tax arrears.

5. Barters and vexels impose high transaction costs. The profit opportunities of the trading intermediaries reduce the profit margin of the producer. They also impose high costs on the economy as prices are not reflective of the true market values of goods. They distort accounts, as investment costs tend to be greatly overstated. This in turn seriously inhibit the efficiency of credit and capital markets. They also enable the hiding of cash flows from the tax authorities. Widespread use of barters and vexels dilute financial controls greatly, and enable transactions, which would not normally be approved under a cash regime. Thus utility managers and staff may incur consumption expenses on facilities and comforts (which would be frowned upon under a cash regime), as the only method of recovering dues from the suppliers of those articles or services.

6. Key areas of reform to reduce the prevalence of barters and vexels include:
- giving energy entities the freedom to cut off supplies to defaulting customers;
- improving bankruptcy and liquidation laws to make them speedy and effective;
- rationalizing the tax structure, removing ambiguities and biases, and adopting better tax collection methods that avoid the routine freezing of the bank accounts of enterprises;
- ensuring a reasonable level of banking confidentiality;
- discouraging the use of higher costs (arising from barters and vexels) for tariff determination by the Energy Regulatory Commissions; and
- introducing a formal regulatory oversight covering the issue and circulation (the number of endorsements) of vexels, and enabling their transparent valuation through appropriate disclosure requirements.
Privatization of the energy entities to strategic investors to achieve more effective corporate governance could also help.

(v) Enabling Disconnection of supply for default

4.17 Utilities all over the world use their right to disconnect supply to defaulting consumers as the key instrument to enforce payment discipline. Like every other effective enforcement mechanism, it should be available as a credible threat to be used sparingly but successfully for the best demonstration effect on the population. Laws must clearly enable the utilities to enforce their contractual right to collect their dues, and refuse to supply to those who default in payments. The laws in Russia, Ukraine and many FSU states are unclear, since new laws contradict old ones (such as the Russian Civil Code), which have not been annulled or amended. The legal validity of the comprehensive instructions for disconnection procedures issued by RAO UES to the regional power companies is open to question. The legal framework both at the federal and regional levels in Russia needs to be addressed to remove ambiguities. Enacting such laws is not perhaps as difficult as preventing the federal and regional politicians from interfering when the utility seeks to disconnect supplies for non-payment. This is clearly a function of the level of political development and the practice of the rule of law. Several East European countries as well as Lithuania and Kazakhstan have made progress in this regard. Armenia is appearing to make major efforts, but claims that it is somewhat hampered by technical difficulties in being able to disconnect customers. The privatized distributing and generating companies in Kazakhstan have made great progress in collections by resorting to imaginative disconnection programs and suspension of

---

Box 4

Good Practices in Relation to Budget Entities

1.   At the beginning of the budget process, the government has to agree with the head of each Ministry / Department on the level of consumption of power, heat and gas for the coming year for each entity under the department. The budget should provide adequate funds as earmarked items to pay for the agreed level of consumption. The relevant utility officials should be associated with these discussions to arrive at realistic estimates of consumption and the required funds to pay for it. The heads of departments should be warned that they should settle promptly the utility bills in full, and that failure to do so would entail the disconnection of service to them under the rules of the utility.

2.   Regarding the stock of past arrears of budget entities, the government should decide on a phased liquidation (including provision of interest on arrears at market rates) and carry out the agreement in a period not exceeding 2 or 3 years. The government may set off the tax arrears of the utility against such past stock of debts of budget entities, but take care to see that such a set off is not used routinely for current dues- as such a practice will induce budget indiscipline in budget entities tempting them to consume more than the agreed level of energy and to divert the funds in the budget for other purposes.

3.   As was done in Lithuania, the government should publish every month a list of heads of departments/offices who failed to pay their bills, or otherwise diverted allocated funds for other purposes, and initiate action to dismiss them for violating budget discipline. Key essential services such as hospitals, fire services, and laboratories could be exempted from being cut off, but their heads of organizations should be subject to dismissal for non-payment. Computerized budget control system should enable the Finance ministry monitor compliance with these requirements continuously and automatically.

4.   This practice must prevail not only in the federal government but also in the regional / provincial and local government levels.

generation. In Russia, Georgia and Ukraine political interference continues unabated and utilities in effect are compelled to supply electricity and natural gas to non-payers. The regional and local politicians harass the utility officials who dare to disconnect. In Albania they threaten to shoot utility officials who attempt to disconnect. In the absence of political maturity and establishment of law and order, one can not envisage any easy solution to the problem.

(vi) Approach to Tariffs

4.18 The historical approach to power tariffs in these countries , by and large, was to enable average tariff to cover the cost of supply. Most of their assets are financed by equity which earns no dividend and is treated as cost free capital. Assets are often valued at their low historical costs without revaluing them to represent replacement costs. In the context of the economic turmoil, some of the FSU countries, such as Russia, allow some revaluation for inflation adjustment. Despite this, the book values of assets continue to be understated, leading to low depreciation expenses. With low or little debt service burden, cost of supply is dominated by variable costs. In fuel import dependent countries, the variable costs quickly rose as a function of international fuel prices, while in countries rich in fuel resources, it rose more as a function of local inflation and with a time lag as a function of traded fuel prices. Since most power systems were characterized by excess capacity and dwindling demand, the long run marginal cost (LRMC) of supply was also modest. Thus all that the governments had to do was to keep the average tariffs above the cost of supply and close to the LRMC and keep on adjusting them for inflation rates and exchange rate variations. In the context of the three digit and four digit inflation experienced in these countries, and devaluation of their currencies by several orders of magnitude, this was no mean task. Further similar adjustments had to be made for tariffs of all other utilities such as heat, water, transport etc., and the cumulative impact of such adjustments was perceived to seriously erode the ability of the consumer to afford even the basic minimum needs. The politicians thus dragged their feet as long as they could, little realizing that if the consumer does not pay the cost, the rest of the economy will have to bear it.

4.19 In addition, power and heat tariff structures in these countries have allowed a high degree of cross subsidization of households by industrial consumers. Price discounts of 50% and 100% had been allowed for a wide range of privileged consumers. Such pricing combined with tolerance of non-payment led to excessive use of power and heat, well beyond the affordable limits of the consumers. Because of inherent inefficiencies the cost of supply from the district heating systems tended to be high. The tariffs had always lagged behind costs and despite this, heavy subsidies from the governments had to be given to the households. The difficulty in the task of adjusting the administered prices to catch up with inflation and rising costs of supply was a function of the relative rates of increases in inflation and personal incomes and political will. Thus it was more difficult in very high inflation countries (Armenia, Georgia, Ukraine, Kazakhstan and Russia) than in countries with relatively lower inflation rates such as Hungary, Poland, Bulgaria, Albania and Lithuania. The question of affordability had to be kept in view all the time. Though the tariff increases appear modest in US dollar terms, the increases expressed in local currency terms were by several orders of magnitude[12], while real incomes of the common people were declining in many of these countries. Thus,

- In Armenia it was estimated in 1992 that if the supply of heat and power were made at tariffs barely adequate to meet the minimum revenue requirements of the utilities, the average household would have to pay 66% of its average monthly income to meet the energy bills. At the tariffs prevailing in 1995, 30% of the households had to spend 20% of their monthly income (of $ 50 or less) on energy;
- In Albania a 1995 survey showed that the bottom 17% of the population would have to spend 14% of their monthly income for power even at the low tariffs prevailing then;
- In Lithuania it was estimated in 1994-95 that households had to pay 26% of the average single salary income for utility services- 3% for power, 15% for heat, and 8% for other utilities. Even at these tariffs, utilities could not recover more than 30% of the supply costs;
- Even in Poland the Office of Statistics estimated that during 1992-93 households paid 9.3% of their disposable income on energy compared to the 3.5% to 4.5% range prevailing in Western Europe.

A study carried out by Bank staff in 1995 in Bulgaria, however, showed that the electricity expenses accounted for only 2.6% of the average household expenses. It was estimated that even a 50% increase in power prices, would raise the consumer price index (CPI) only by 1.25%, while the financial burden of not raising the tariff would exceed 1.5% of GDP. This study also showed that keeping the power prices low for all consumers did not necessarily help the poor. It showed that in fact the wealthiest 10% of the households got 67% more subsidy than the poorest 10%.

4.20 Available power tariff information in these countries is summarized in Table 5 below.

Table 5: Power Tariffs in Select East European and FSU Countries
(In US Cents/kWh)

Country	Year	Average Tariff	Households Tariff	Industrial Tariff
Albania	1993	1.40	0.8 to 3.0	..
	1995	4.00	4.74	3.50
	1998	3.36	3.20	2.00
Bulgaria	1990	2.39	1.10	2.50
	1992	..	1.40	2.20
	1998	3.25	2.91	4.56
Hungary	1986	2.01	1.25	2.25
	1994		5.50	5.20
	1998	5.83	6.25	5.60
Poland	1994	..	5.10	3.70

---

[12] According to Goskomstat, electricity prices in Russia are estimated to have risen by 4897 times during 1991-96.

	1995	5.50	5.50	4.00
	1997	6.20	..	..
Lithuania	1993	2.00	1.0 to 2.0	1.0 to 3.0
	1995	3.50	3.95	3.29
	1996	4.00	4.21	3.45
Armenia	1994	1.40	0.40	2.40
	1997	4.20	4.40	4.00
	1998[13]	5.10	5.30	4.80
Georgia	1996	2.42	1.80	3.20
	1997	3.40	3.40	3.40
Russia	1994	..	0.60	2.70
	1997	..	1.80	4.2 to 6.2
Ukraine	1994	1.30	0.34	1.40
	1995	2.50	2.4 to 2.8	2.4 to 2.7
	1996	3.90	4.4 to 4.7	4.0 to 4.3
Kazakhstan	1998	4.40	4.00	4.75

Source: WB Internal Documents

In Bulgaria, Albania, Hungary and Poland tariffs are believed to cover supply costs and to be close to LRMC. In Russia, Lithuania, Kazakhstan they are believed to be close to supply costs. In Armenia and Ukraine further adjustments may be required to cover supply costs. A comparison of Table 5 above and Table 2 on the Status of Non-payments suggests that adjustment of tariffs and reduction of internal cross subsidies do not necessarily lead to poor collections. In Bulgaria, Lithuania, Hungary, Poland, and even in Armenia, tariff increases have coexisted with collection improvements. Surveys in Armenia have shown that people tend to pay the bills when they perceive the service quality to be acceptable. Cost recovering tariffs enable utilities to improve the quality of service, which in turn promotes better payment performance. Thus it would appear that the key approach to tariffs is their timely adjustment to cover supply costs and to minimize internal cross subsidies.

---

[13] This tariff level is expected to be operational only from January 1999.

(vii) Approach to subsidies

4.21 As long as poverty exists, subsidies can not perhaps be entirely eliminated. They can certainly be made efficient, explicit, quantifiable and targeted to reach the specified poverty group. Lowering the prices for households as a whole and providing 50% and 100% discounts to privileged classes are inefficient and costly, apart from the fact that they do not necessarily protect the poor. Keeping prices at cost recovery levels and

---

Box 5

SMALLER OR BIGGER DISTRIBUTION COMPANIES?

1.   In the context of poor overall collections and even poorer cash collections in the FSU countries, the question that came up often is whether for the given country, there should be a larger or smaller number of distribution companies to achieve a greater efficiency of collection. Associated questions are whether one should encourage or eliminate resellers and whether power distribution, as in the case of heat distribution, be decentralized to the municipal level.

2.   The argument for larger number of distribution entities, decentralizing power distribution to municipalities or for encouraging resellers is that such an arrangement will bring the entity closer to the consumers and enable it to monitor collection more intensively and at least in the case of municipalities, popularly elected local politicians would be more effective in persuading their constituents to pay the power bills promptly. The example of Denmark with over 100 distribution companies is often cited as a good example.

3.   Available evidence in the countries under consideration does not seem to validate these postulates. The organization of three small privatized pilot distribution companies in Albania did not lead to any better collection performance. In fact their collection deteriorated so fast, that the government is considering reabsorbing them in KESH and organizing larger and viable companies. In Georgia, when the sector was unbundled and 66 regional distribution companies were formed, 51 of them were turned over to the municipalities in mid 1995. This did not result in any improved collection performance for the sector. Though the distribution companies did collect a little more than in the past, they did not pay Sakenergo (the grid company which buys power from the generators and sells it to the distribution companies) properly for power purchases. Their debts to Sakenergo rose from about $102 million in 1996 to $ 147 million in 1997. Similar results have taken place in several regions of Russia, and in the pilot project at Zezkazgan oblast in Kazakhstan, in all of which municipal distribution companies and resellers provide yet another layer of "money changers" in the power sector, providing yet another opportunity for the disappearance of cash from the system. The closeness of the elected municipal officials to the people in effect leads to their inability to disconnect defaulters.

4.   The government of Georgia is now considering a proposal to regroup the 66 distribution companies into four large viable companies and privatize them. Similar reduction in the number of distribution entities have taken place in Armenia (from 70 to 11), and Bulgaria (28 to 15). Komi region in Russia has taken over all the municipal systems and has practically eliminated most of the resellers. Many other regions are eliminating resellers as a matter of policy. The experiment in Armenia using consumer cooperatives or consumer associations was not a success.. In Kazakhstan suggestions have been made to reduce the number of distribution entities from 15 (excluding the three already privatized) to a smaller number of more viable entities.

5.   On the whole in the power sector, which unlike the heat supply sector, operates as an interconnected system throughout the country, the key is to organize institutions based on economies of scale (typically with one million consumers or 2500 to 3000 GWh of sales), which has to be balanced with logistics of movement and control. Given the size of the power systems of many of these countries, there is no compelling reason to increase the number of distribution entities. Consolidation of existing entities into viable units with economies of scale and providing them with good corporate governance seems to be the right thing to do. Decentralization of heat distribution entities to the municipal level may be appropriate, as it is essentially a decentralized technical operation and as it can be regarded as a municipal service. This is clearly not the case in respect of power distribution. When the population of a municipal area is large enough to provide economies of scale, it may be appropriate to organize power distribution systems to be coterminous with municipal boundaries. Mosenergo in Russia and Kievenergo in Ukraine are good examples of this. In actual practice many such companies organized originally that way expand to cover the surrounding suburban areas as well. There is however no special reason for such a company to be owned by the municipality. It is perhaps best to organize it as a private company with good corporate governance.

subsidizing directly (not through the utility) the target poverty group is clearly a more efficient solution. Thus

- Reflecting the cost of supply, Lithuania adopted in 1996 heat prices for households slightly higher than those for industries and provided direct subsidies to the households spending more than 15% of their household income on space heating and more than 5% of their income on hot water;
- Bulgaria introduced a means tested energy voucher system based on the size of the apartment and the number of occupants, enabling those with income up to 150% of the nationally defined basic minimum income level to get graduated subsidy in the form of energy vouchers which they could use to pay for power, heat or coal. Such an approach helped to solve simultaneously the utility viability problem, payment problem and social protection problem;
- Hungary set up in 1997, a Social Compensation Fund with HUF 1.0 billion from the government budget and HUF 0.5 billion from MVM Rt (the Grid company) and the privatized distribution companies. In 1998 the size of the Fund was HUF 800 million- half of it coming from the utilities and the other half from the budget. The fund will be used to provide HUF 1700 to 12,000 per year to about 380,000 specifically identified poor households to compensate them for the high energy tariffs not affordable by them;
- Armenia adopted a life line rate for households consuming less than 100 kWh per month, gave up the practice of giving discounts to privileged classes of consumers and started providing direct subsidy to a narrowly defined poverty group.

Ukraine, Georgia, Kazakhstan and Russia have to move in this direction to reform their approach to subsidies.

(viii) Decentralization

4.22 Decentralization of the provision of district heating services to the municipal level, as has been done in Lithuania, Poland, Hungary and several energos of Russia, could perhaps be considered a practical option, since district heating, unlike power supply, is a decentralized activity in any case. The approach could be the same as in the case of other urban services such as water supply, sewerage, sanitation, local transport and parks. However, decentralizing electricity supply to the municipal levels may not be appropriate, unless the size of the population in the municipality could provide economies of scale, say 1.0 million customers or 2500 to 3000 GWh of annual sales (See Box 5 on Smaller or Bigger Distribution companies). Experience in Georgia, Russia and Armenia clearly indicate the negative consequences of decentralizing power distribution to municipal levels.

Box 6

VERTICALLY INTEGRATED OR UNBUNDLED POWER SECTOR?

1.   What kind of power sector structure is preferred from the point of view of overcoming the payment problem? A vertically integrated utility? or an unbundled set of power sector institutions? The case studies and other examples from the East Europe and FSU states do not seem to provide a clear answer to these questions.

2.   Lithuania, Bulgaria, and Albania operate in the traditional mode, in which LPC, NEK, and KESH respectively operate as vertically integrated power companies. The overall performance as well as collection performance are acceptable in LPC and NEK and poor in KESH. Even the experimental unbundling and privatization attempted in three small pilot distribution companies in Albania had a poor overall record and a poorer collection performance.

3.   Armenia, Hungary, Georgia, Kazakhstan, Poland, and Ukraine operate unbundled power systems. Poland and Hungary have excellent overall performance and presently have no significant collection or payment related problem. Armenia and Kazakhstan are trying to improve their performance under the unbundled structures, but find that unbundling has created new collection problems in the sector. Georgia is clearly not an example to prove that unbundled power sector structure improves payment performance in the sector. The Russian Energos handle generation, transmission at 220 kV and below, as well as distribution and should be regarded as vertically integrated within their region. Their performance is mixed. Their collection performance, especially their cash collection performance is distinctly deplorable. The exceptions seem to be the energos based in metropolitan areas such as Moscow and Kiev. The collection performance of both Hungary and Poland were good both when they had vertically integrated utilities and when they changed over to unbundled utilities.

4.   The only possible conclusion under these circumstances is that from the point of view of solving the non-payment problem, what really matters is good corporate governance and not the type of structure. In the absence of good corporate governance, unbundling by itself does not do any good. In fact there is evidence that it creates more intractable problems. The reason for advocating unbundling, is that it could facilitate privatization paving the way for good corporate governance by the private sector. For the unbundling to succeed two key conditions must be met. First the method of privatizing should result in the company acquiring strong corporate governance. Privatization to qualified and competent strategic investors, as was done in Hungary or Kazakhstan usually results in this. Privatization done in Albania or Russia to managers and staff through vouchers or mass privatization clearly does not achieve this objective. Second, there must be a strong and well rooted convention and tradition of abiding by contractual obligations and quick, inexpensive and impartial methods(arbitration, courts, orders of the regulator, and the like) of enforcing contractual rights between companies. In the absence of such a tradition and framework, the contracts among the generating companies, transmission companies and distribution companies become mere pieces of ineffective paper, resulting in the collections of the distribution companies not being passed on to the transmission and generating companies, thus creating serious sector viability problems.

5. Thus in Georgia, Armenia, Ukraine and Kazakhstan we witness the situation of the distribution companies accumulating huge debts to the grid companies and generators. They retain whatever they collect and pass on only a portion of their collection up the ladder in gross violation of the power purchase agreements. A firm tradition of the distribution companies financing their working capital needs by defaulting on their payments to the grid companies seem to have set in. If in this context, generating companies and distribution companies are privatized, it could result in the publicly owned grid company being totally squeezed out for resources. In fact such a situation has already arisen in Kazakhstan, where the state owned grid company KEGOC is contemplating whether the power supply to the defaulting distribution company should be disconnected. Similar problems have arisen often in Russia where resellers collect the dues from the consumers and do not pass on the collections to the power company. Russian regional power companies which buy electricity from the generating subsidiaries of RAO UES through the wholesale power market (FOREM), either do not pay for the power purchased or pay only through barter, vexel or set off, thereby effectively stopping the flow of cash to RAO UES and its generating subsidiaries.

6.   The dilemma in such cases is whether it is proper to deny power supply to the resellers or distribution companies as a whole and penalize the paying customers for the fault of the intermediary. The legal position would be that the contract must be enforced and power supply cut off to the distribution company. Common sense, however dictates that our arrangements must provide meaningful alternatives to the paying end users without necessarily asking them to relocate to another franchise area!! Russia is trying, as a matter of public policy, to get rid of the institution of resellers. But distribution companies once created are difficult to get rid of. Legal mechanisms must enable a swift take over of such companies. Before deciding to unbundle the sector these aspects should be carefully taken into account.

(ix) Approach to Restructuring and Privatization

4.23 A review of the case studies suggests that there is no straight forward relationship between the non-payment problem and the issues relating to sector restructuring and privatization (see Box 6 on Vertically Integrated or unbundled Power Sector?). Government ownership of vertically integrated utilities has clearly been conducive to the tolerance of non-payment culture, as the roles of ownership, regulation, and management are blurred and mutually compromised. It has provided governments a tempting opportunity to achieve fiscal balances by tolerating non-payments in the energy sector. The question, however, is whether sector unbundling, corporatization and privatization should be undertaken to get rid of non-payment problem or whether non-payment problem should be overcome first to enable successful privatization. The case studies do not provide material for a clear resolution of this question. Kazakhstan abruptly privatized its generation companies and some distribution companies with remarkable results on its payment situation[14]. Hungary, Poland, Lithuania and Bulgaria solved the payment problem first, which enabled them to proceed in an orderly fashion in the direction of corporatization, commercialization, sector unbundling and towards meaningful and effective privatization. The type of privatization done in Albania, Russia and other FSU countries only worsened the payment situation, as it did not provide any effective corporate governance. The only lesson that stands out is this: that the fight against non-payment problem can be won by a vertically integrated utility, an unbundled utility, a government owned utility or a private utility-- as long as it gets effective and meaningful corporate governance with arms length relationship from the government. In the absence of such governance, none of the above forms succeed.

4.24 Some general recommendations on the sequence of reform are also possible. Corporatization and commercialization must be done as a first step in any case to create the legal entity separate from the government, separate its assets and liabilities from those of the government, enable independent accounting and audit etc. and to be able to track meaningfully the effect of steps taken. Some governments were able to deal with such corporatized entities at an arms length and provide disciplined corporate governance (examples are Lithuania, Bulgaria, Hungary, and Poland) and managed to solve the non-payment problem in this environment. After stabilizing the cash flows of the entity at reasonable levels, meaningful privatization to strategic investors to ensure even better corporate governance should be undertaken to sell the assets at values close to their true potential. In a number of countries, however, this arms length relationship has failed to develop suggesting that a change in ownership arrangements is needed to improve corporate governance. The example of Tractebel S.A., in Almatyenergo of Kazakhstan show the improvements due to the presence of a strategic investor, as well as the advantages of rebundling power and heat supply from the point of view of collection efficiency. Sector unbundling alone, in the absence of good corporate governance and firmly rooted commercial practices protected by effective contractual rights enforcement

---

[14] It is widely believed, based on the statements of the buyers, that Kazakhstan sold its assets at throw away prices. This is inevitable since buyers only look at the present value of future cash flows projected mainly on the basis of present extremely poor cash flows.

systems, will not solve (and may even aggravate) the non-payment problem and non-cash payment problem, as can be readily seen from the examples of Ukraine, Armenia, Georgia, and Russia.[15]

(x) Regulation

4.25 Another key task for governments is to provide impartial, independent and competent sector regulation and free the process of tariff setting from political interference. Regulation intended to promote competition in relevant segments, to determine tariffs for the natural monopolistic elements, to resolve sector disputes, and to oversee the adherence of the sector entities to the prescribed grid code, safety and environment norms is a key component in the march of these nations to market economy. Most of the countries in the Central and Eastern Europe and FSU have created regulatory bodies, with varying degrees of independence, effectiveness and competence. There is clear evidence that governments still tend to interfere in the decisions of even the most capable of regulatory bodies. These institutions are young and with the maturation of the democratic politics of these countries, could be expected to become gradually effective. The governments have to learn to leave them alone.

---

[15] Letter of credit arrangements for supplies to large consumers and escrow account mechanisms to ensure a timely and fair flow of funds from the collections of the distribution utility to the transmission and generation entities and to fuel suppliers would be examples of good contracting mechanisms. Efficient banking services would be a great help in this regard.

5. LESSONS FOR THE BANK

A. Approach to Lending and Non-Lending Services

5.1   A review of the situation in East European and FSU countries clearly indicates that the problems of non-payment and non-cash payment occur economy wide and are not confined to the energy sector alone. The solution to these problems is linked to a range of key economic variables such as GDP growth, inflation, exchange rate regimes, taxation, income distribution, and social protection. Successful efforts to overcome the problem have to encompass industrial restructuring, banking reform, enterprise reform and privatization, creation and improvement of legal infrastructure and public administrative reform and address the key cross-cutting issues of corruption and governance, besides stabilization measures. Energy sector reform by itself, will not rectify the problem. The situation is best addressed by a combination of structural adjustment and sector adjustment lending in conjunction with carefully designed energy investment lending (mainly to enlist the active cooperation of the energy entities) covering the above areas, preceded by a thorough and detailed analysis. Both the analysis to precede the loans and the TAs to accompany the loans require significant resources to be devoted to the use of consultants in the field working with the utility staff. In view of the reluctance of borrowers to apply loan funds for TA activity, the Bank has to mobilize substantial grant funds and also to work closely with other lenders and donors to evolve common and well coordinated TA programs administered with a single purpose and common goal. The example of the work done in Russian power sector for the reform of regional energos and regional regulatory bodies seems to be a good example. Similarly the adjustment lending operations done in Lithuania and Armenia seem to provide good examples for addressing the non-payment issue in the energy sector, while covering all the related issues.

5.2   The Bank's contribution to the design of the stabilization programs should help to establish clear macro-micro linkages and to ensure that government budget deficits and quasi budget deficits (such as the deficits of government owned banks, enterprises, energy entities and where relevant, the social security system) are effectively tackled to avoid the situation of fiscal balance being achieved at the cost of accumulating huge arrears to, and capital consumption in, the energy sector. The work done in Lithuania seems to be a good example, but further close coordination between IMF and the Bank would appear to be necessary. The conditionalities under the IMF operations need to include settlement of energy sector payments (both dues owed to the energy entities and taxes owed by them to government) and social safety nets.

5.3   The energy sector analytical work and lending must address the non-payment issue, but it should also encompass sector viability concerns (external subsidies, returns on assets, internal generation of cash for rehabilitation needs) and tariff concerns (structure, levels, internal cross subsidies, targeted support for the poorer sections, social safety net) in order not to lose sight of the perennial concerns, while dealing with what is, hopefully, a transient problem. Dilemmas arise, when, as in Russia, the government offers 50% discount to those who pay in cash. While it may or may not encourage cash payment, it would certainly cut into sector viability, since most utilities can not afford to lose 50% of their revenue[16]. Such adventurous measures belong to the microeconomic systems of the private sector, where the investor bears the consequences of his decision. In the public domain, where the exit gates are firmly locked, these choices will have to be carefully thought through. To be able to respond to developments like this, the Bank needs to be involved with a lending portfolio with appropriate coverage.

B. Approach to Sector Restructuring and Privatization

5.4   As discussed in Chapter 4, the approach to restructuring of the power sector needs to be pragmatic. There is no single ideal sequencing of the steps of reform (such as corporatizing, commercializing, sector unbundling, regulation, privatization and the introduction of competition) applicable to all countries. The sequence appropriate to each country will have to be determined based on the country circumstances. In large countries such as Russia, the approach may even have to vary for different parts of the country.[17] Examples of Hungary, Poland, Bulgaria and Lithuania demonstrate that, with a measure of disciplined arms length corporate governance, state owned vertically integrated utilities can overcome their operational problems and make themselves ready for restructuring and privatization to achieve greater levels of efficiency through competition. Privatization to strategic investors as an initial step after sector unbundling and corporatization to solve the problems of the sector seem to have met with some success in Kazakhstan. However half hearted privatization, which does not bring in any measure of good corporate governance and which merely results in "insider domination", as in many FSU countries creates more problems. Sector unbundling can actually cause serious aggravation of the non-payment problem, if the culture of enforcing contract compliance is not fully developed and made to take root. The examples of Russia, Georgia, Ukraine, and Armenia come readily to the mind as the distribution companies there did not pass on fully, the collections they made, thus starving the transmission and generation companies for funds. Privatization is best started with distribution systems and then moved to cover generation and eventually, if practical, to transmission and load dispatch. But efforts to privatize the sector must be accompanied by strong contract enforcement systems and dispute resolution systems . The importance of impartial and independent regulation in this context can not be overemphasized.

C. Clear Focus on Federal / Regional / Local Inter- Relationships

5.5   The Bank should continue to study the inter-relationship among the federal, regional and local governments to develop an understanding of the existing arrangements, their strength and weaknesses and implications to Bank operations in individual sectors or across the sectors. In Russia, and in many federated states, this is a key problem area. Interference by regional and local politicians with energy sector agencies is at the bottom of most of the problems. The design of the sector structure, ownership patterns and responsibilities should be in consonance with the political structures to avoid perpetual

---

[16] The decree also stipulates that in any case the discounted price should not be lower than the cost of generation and transmission. It is somewhat difficult to see how this can be achieved.

[17] Such an approach has been adopted in the reform program for the Russian power sector, recently formulated by RAO UES.

conflicts. The design of nation wide energy systems and local energy systems and their inter-relationship should be in consonance with the political systems. The aim should be to promote relationships based on substantial decentralization of responsibility in appropriate spheres, matching it with appropriate delegation of powers and devolution of resources. The analytical work of the Bank should be geared to review these relationships for the political administration as a whole and for each major sector and adjustment and investment lending should be designed to focus on the recommended improvements.

PART II

CASE STUDIES

THE ALBANIAN CASE STUDY

A. Macroeconomic Developments

1.   Albania, with a population of about 3.3 million and an annual per capita GNP of about $ 830, is one of the poorest countries in Europe. Its GDP declined by about 40% during 1990-1992. During this period its overall fiscal deficit rose to the level of 22% of GDP, broad money ranged between 70% and 55% of GDP and its annual inflation rate rose to 240% in 1992. Unemployment touched a high of 24%. Exchange rate moved from 10 Leks to 90 Leks per dollar, current account deficit rose to a level of 65% of GDP, and foreign exchange reserves sank to levels equivalent to less than one month's imports.

2.   Stabilization efforts taken since then resulted in remarkable improvements. A real annual GDP growth of about 9% was achieved during 1993-1996, inflation came down to about 6% and fiscal deficit came down to 10-12% of GDP by early 1996. Unemployment was halved to 12%. Exchange rate appreciated during 1994 and 1995 and exchange reserves rose to a level equivalent to 3 month's imports. However the major political unrest and violence following the collapse of the pyramid schemes in 1996 reversed these happy trends. In 1997 GDP fell by 10% and inflation rose to 42%. Remittances from overseas declined and capital flight from Albania took place and exchange rate declined by 40%. The country was under an IMF program for six months (November 1997- April 1998) followed by a three year ESAF program of IMF (1998-2001) following tight fiscal and monetary polices to bring down inflation to 4%, fiscal deficits to 6% by 2001, while achieving about 7% to 8% annual GDP growth. Fiscal deficits are to be brought down largely by cutting down government expenditure and partly by raising revenues by excise duty.

B. Impact on the Power Sector

3.   Albania operates a modest sized power system with a total installed power generation capacity of 1659 MW, which consists of 11 hydroelectric stations (1446 MW) and 7 thermal power plants (213 MW). The economic decline in the 1990-92 period, and the collapse of trading arrangements under CEMA led to a fall in the industrial output with adverse impact on the power sector. Gross generation declined[18] from 4154 Gwh in 1989 to 3353 Gwh in 1992. Domestic consumption and sales also correspondingly declined. During the entire period 1989-94, the industrial demand declined, while the demand from the households registered a steady growth, induced by the use of appliances sent or financed by relatives abroad. On account of the demand growth coming mainly from households, peak demand had been rising, and system load factor falling, rapidly during the last several years (see Table 1). The most significant development was the steep increase in the total system losses[19] from 13.2% in 1989 to 48.7% in 1994 and to

---

[18] The decline in generation is also attributable to poor hydrology in the year.

[19] Total system loss = (Gross Generation - exports - Domestic sales) = Losses in Generation, Transmission and Distribution segments of the business.

57% in 1997. While the auxiliary consumption by the generating stations at 0.5% is reasonable, the transmission losses at 14.3% are very high for such a small system as that of Albania and are attributed to the overloading of the system and the change in the structure of demand from predominantly industrial loads to predominantly household loads[20]. The losses at the distribution level were at an alarmingly high level of 50.7% consisting of technical losses (16.3%) and non-technical losses (34.4%)-- the latter arising mainly from theft of electricity (mostly by households and small industrial and commercial consumers), defective metering, and billing assumptions regarding levels of consumption for unmetered supplies, which are no longer valid.

Table 1: Power System Changes in Albania

Item	1989	1992	1994	1997
Gross Generation (Gwh)	4154	3353	3904	5182
Net exports (Gwh)	640	560	185	128
Domestic Demand (Gwh)	3514	2793	3719	5054
Losses in Generation (Gwh)	74	44	38	27
(as a % of gross generation)	(1.8%)	(1.3%)	(1%)	(0.5%)
Losses in Transmission (Gwh)	306	327	452	739
(as a % of gross generation)	(7.4%)	(9.8%)	(11.6%)	(14.2%)
Losses in Distribution (Gwh)	163	769	1391	2174
(as a % of gross generation)	(4%)	(23%)	(35.6%)	(42%)
Total Losses as a % of Gross Generation	13.2	34.1	48.2	57
Total Sales (Gwh)	2971	1653	1838	2114
Peak Demand (MW)	596	640	801	..
System Load Factor (%)	67	50	54	..

Source: WB Internal Documents

High technical losses at the transmission and distribution levels are sought to be reduced to normal levels by undertaking rehabilitation and reinforcement of the T&D system under financing by the Bank and other donors. The problem of non-technical losses, however, continues to be intractable.

4.   During the period 1989 -1994 the composition of the power demand has also changed significantly, as in the case of other East European and FSU countries. The share of the households in the energy sales rose from 9% in 1989 to 42% in 1994, while the share of industry and mines dropped from 49% to 29% during the same period. It declined further to 23% by 1997 (see Table 2 below). In terms of sales values in 1997, the share of households was the highest at 51.4% followed by government owned non-budget entities -mostly state owned industrial and mining enterprises- (29.5%), other private consumers (12.4%) and government budget entities (6.8%). Simultaneously, collection of dues from consumers have been falling steeply and was at the level of 53% of billing in 1997. Thus the country was not able to convert more than 23% of the power generated into revenues.

---

[20] One suspects, however, that it may be attributable partly to measurement and allocation problems in a vertically integrated utility.

Table 2: Changes in the Composition of Power Demand

Item	1989	1992	1994
Total Sales (Gwh)	2971	1653	1838
Share of Households (%)	9	29	42
Share of Industry and Mines (%)	49	30	29
Share of others (%)	42	41	29

Source: WB Internal Documents

C. Collection Performance

5.   The steady decline in collection performance in respect of four key categories of consumers is summarized in Table 3 for the years 1995-1997.

Table 3: Collection Performance in the Power Sector
(as a % of billing in the year)

Category	1995	1996	1997
Households	91	84	72
Other Private Sector Consumers	92	91	90
Government Budget Entities	109	63	59
Government Owned Non-budget Entities	53	52	21
Total for all Categories	79	71	53
Total for KESH without Pilot Companies	79	72	58
Total for Pilot Companies Only	--	55	10

Source: WB Internal Documents

Note: 1. The Pilot Companies are those organized at Elbasan, Shkoder and Vlore as semi privatized Joint stock companies in September 1995. The data given probably relates to the amounts payable by the pilot companies to KESH, rather than to their own collection performance.
      2. KESH is the vertically integrated state owned power utility distributing power in all other areas. It is also responsible for generation, transmission and load dispatch.

As a result, the accounts receivable, at the end of 1997, rose to a staggeringly high level equivalent to 11 months of energy sales. The largest share of the accounts receivable was from government owned non-budget entities (49%) and from households (40%), as can be seen from Table 4. Among the government owned non-budget entities, Albkrom (chromium mining and processing enterprise), Albpetrol (petroleum enterprise) and Water supply enterprises accounted for most of the arrears. Among the government budget entities the arrears from the ministries of interior, irrigation and radio and television were prominent.

Table 4: Accounts Receivable Situation in Albania.
(amounts in Leks million)

Item	Accounts Receivable as of 31.12.96	1997 Billings	1997 Collections	1997 Collection (%)	Accounts Receivable as of 31.12.97	In Months of 1997 Billings
Households	1723	3956 (51.4%)	2853	72	2826 (40%)	9
Other Private	224	952 (12.4%)	854	90	322 (4.5%)	4
Government Budget Entities	238	525 (6.8%)	308	59	455 (6.5%)	10
Government Non-Budget Entities	1668	2270 (29.5%)	475	21	3463 (49%)	21
Total	3857	7703 (100%)	4490	58	7070 (100%)	11

Source: WB Internal Documents

D. Approach to Tariffs

6.   Tariffs for households were at the level of US cents 0.5 /kWh in 1992. They were later raised to the level of Cents 0.8 /kWh and the average for all consumers remained at about Cents 1.9 /kWh till the end of March 1994. As a part of the reforms undertaken to stabilize the economy, power prices, like all other energy prices were adjusted upwards somewhat steeply. With effect from April 1, 1994, the average tariff /kWh for all consumers rose to the level of Cents 4.0 and household tariffs / kWh rose to the level of Cents 4.8 (corresponding to Leks 4.5 /kWh). The tariff level compares with LRMC at about Cents 7.5 /kWh. Presently the average tariff is at 4.8 Leks/kWh including a VAT of 20%, though in US cents terms it has fallen to 3.3 /kWh on account of the devaluation of Lek in 1998. However the tendency to steal electricity was evident even before the rate increases, which may have made it more attractive and widespread. The steep rise in tariffs may have been partly responsible for the non-payment by households. Based on aggregate level statistics, even if the entire gross electricity generation in the country in 1997 is paid for at the rate of 4.8 Leks/kWh, the per capita annual electricity bill would be 7536 Leks (or $51) or 7.33% of per capita GDP[21]. This does not appear to be too high a level, except perhaps in the case of the lowest 20% of the population classified as poor. Such an analysis based on aggregate data could however be misleading. Price increases have taken place simultaneously in respect of all other fuels such as oil products, coal, LPG and fuel wood. A household energy survey carried out in 1995 indicated that the top 14% of the population earning over 8000 Leks/month spent only 6% of their income on energy, while the bottom 17% earning less than 3000 Leks/month spent 14% of their income on energy. A more detailed survey and household expenditure analysis would be needed to determine whether the price increases should have been staggered.   The government did increase the wages, pension, unemployment benefits and welfare benefits

---

[21] Based on estimates of 1997 nominal GDP and exchange rates given in the Albania Policy Framework Paper (30 April 1998) and power system statistics.

simultaneously to provide some relief to the population. Such increased benefits were financed out of the tax component of the power tariffs. This however is an inefficient mechanism, since the benefits do not reach exclusively the target group. It is also worth noting that tariffs for state owned heavy industries and bakeries the tariffs have been kept very low (Leks 3.0 and 1.2 respectively per kWh), compared to private sector MV and LV consumers at Leks 5.3 and 6.3 respectively.

E. Sector Organization

7. KESH is the vertically integrated state owned power utility responsible for generation, transmission and distribution through out the country except in three small areas, where separate small joint stock companies for distribution have been set up since September 1995. It reports to the Ministry of Public Economy and Privatization, which appoints the 9 member council to supervise KESH. KESH is organized in the form of 9 generation and transmission enterprises and 35 distribution enterprises. I t employs about 9400 persons with monthly average salaries in the range of $ 152 to $ 373 . Government has enacted in the course of 1995 a series of laws relating the power sector- the Electricity Law, Privatization of Energy Law, Regulation of Electricity Sector Law, Concessions Law etc. A three member Regulatory Agency as an offshoot of MPEP has also been created to handle price regulation in Power sector.

F. Incentive Scheme for Staff

8. To reduce theft of electricity and to collect the arrears, a wide range of technical and institutional measures, including the establishment in 1994 of the Electricity Inspectorate, were adopted. Two of these are noteworthy in the context of a regional study. The first was an incentive scheme operated by KESH. Teams were set up for each distribution feeder, the electrical input into which could be metered. The team for each such feeder was given a target for loss reduction and when it met or exceeded the target, the members were given as bonus a sum equivalent to 50% of the value of loss reduction at bulk supply prices, subject to the condition that the bonus for any employee would not exceed 50% of his salary. If the team failed to meet the target, the salary for its members for the period was reduced and could fall to the minimum level of 4000 Leks/month. In respect of Distribution Managers, 10% of their base salary was retained . When they met the targets they got back not only the retained 10%, but a bonus of another 10% of their salary. If they failed to meet the target, they lost their retained 10%. The scheme was introduced in 1995 and appeared to succeed initially. It was, however, given up sometime during the next year on account of two developments. First, measurement problems on the feeders arose. Second, in a dispute between KESH and its staff, the court held that the staff could not be held responsible for theft of electricity by consumers and that their salaries could not be cut. Theft of power on such a large scale would not be possible without some cooperation from some of the corrupt officials of KESH. While KESH had to discontinue the above incentive scheme, it had been following the policy of dismissing the officials identified as engaged in such corrupt practices. This needs to be kept up, and ways of reviving a properly designed incentive scheme should be explored.

G. Partial Privatization of Distribution

9.   The second strategy was to privatize electricity distribution under the belief that Albanians tend to treat services provided by the state as free, while they respected private property rights. Three pilot distribution areas-- Elbasan, Shkoder and Vlore-- were separated from KESH and set up as three joint stock companies. Thirty percent of their shares were auctioned following the procedures of "mass or voucher privatization" and the shares are widely held, with the workers in these companies holding about 5% of the shares. A majority of the remaining shares was to be given to a strategic investor, but so far none has been identified. The pilot companies were unable to show any improvement. In fact their cumulative performance turned out to be well below that of KESH (see Table 3). They lacked economies of scale and had no superior management input. Their half hearted privatization did not change the character of the company and did not bring any added value. Suggestions have been made to merge them back with KESH and consolidate the distribution enterprises into a small number of viable entities, before privatizing them to strategic investors. For the present the government is considering the transfer of its shares in the three pilot companies to KESH.

H. Approach to Government Budget Entities

10.   The country had been under IMF Standby arrangements during 1992-1993 and under ESAF during 1993-96. At the Bank's request towards the end of 1995, all the accounts receivable by KESH from government budget entities and non-budgetary entities, as well as the tax arrears of KESH to Government were written off. Despite this , the level of arrears from them exceeds the equivalent of 10 months energy sales to them With the cooperation of IMF under ESAF II, the Bank had been persuading the government to settle periodically the arrears of government budget entities, through earmarked allocations, direct adjustments and adjustments against VAT dues from KESH. The government has recently instructed all government budget entities and non budget entities (except water supply companies and hospitals) to settle in full the bills for the six month period Oct. 97 to March 98 before 14 April and has authorized KESH to disconnect the defaulters. This has resulted in some noteworthy improvements in respect of collection from the government budget entities[22]. The country is under ESAF II during May 1998- May 2001. The key objective of this ESAF program is bring down the inflation rate from 11% to 4% and the domestically financed fiscal deficit from about 11% to 3% of GDP. The focus is primarily on improving the revenue collection efficiency and improve receipts and on tight money policy. Under this program close coordination with IMF needs to be maintained to ensure that that the budget entities are provided with adequate earmarked resources to settle their arrears to public utilities and to pay their current dues. A review of the economy wide inter agency arrears for this purpose should be undertaken.

---

[22] The collection rate for GBEs improved from 59% in 1997 to 127% in January-August 1998. The rate for all consumers increased from 53% to 78%.

I. State Owned Enterprises

11.   The problem of non-payment by government owned non-budget organizations such as Albkrom, Albpetrol and the Water supply enterprises has proved to be even more intractable. In the case of Albpetrol, which supplies heavy fuel oil to KESH, periodic mutual adjustments of accounts payable and accounts receivable seems to alleviate the problem to some extent. It is somewhat strange that an oil company is not solvent enough to pay its bills. Outdated technologies, poor quality of its products and poor management appear to have eroded its financial viability. While the government is committed to its privatization, the progress had been slow. Proposals to provide an adequately funded technical assistance to the Government to privatize this company need to be followed up.

12.   From the point of view of electricity arrears, the need to privatize or close down Albkrom is even more urgent. Albkrom is a power intensive industry which appears to consume about 12 to 14 GWh of energy every month valued at around 60 million Leks. Non-payment of its annual energy bills amounting 720 million Leks (or $4.9 million) is perhaps the largest single drain from the resources of the power sector. The company faces difficult geological conditions, expensive mining operations, outdated technology and major market fluctuations. During the collapse of the economy, mineral exports were the hardest hit[23], and the sector has not recovered yet. The government has been pursuing the privatization of this company for over for over 4 years now with some potential foreign joint venture partners (under EBRD assistance), but had not so far been successful. The Albanian Policy Framework Paper (April 1998) envisages the privatization of Albkrom and Albpetrol within the current ESAF period[24]. Assistance to the government in this regard may deserve high priority.

13.   Water supply enterprises seem to have a price cap tariff fixed at a level which barely covers 50% of the supply cost. Thus they do not generate adequate revenues to pay their bills fully or on schedule. In the context of a water supply operation, the Bank is reviewing whether the government could raise the price cap to enable a better level of cost recovery. However, the cumulative impact of rate increases both in the energy and water sectors on the poorer households has to be examined carefully before taking a decision in the matter. In the event of KESH having to write off the arrears from water utilities, the government needs to refund the VAT collected from KESH on such sales. The present practice of the government collecting VAT on all billed sales irrespective of whether the bill is paid or not, is appropriate, but refund procedures for sales in respect of which dues could not be recovered have to be developed.

J. Approach to Households

14.   Theft of power through illegal connections or by tampering with the installed meters by the households and small private enterprises is the most serious problem in Albania, which needs to be tackled effectively within the framework of social dynamics

---

[23] Mineral exports fell from $141 million in 1989 to $18..3 million in 1992.

[24] Three years from mid May 1998.

and security environment of the country. In many countries the power company's authority to disconnect power supply is difficult to exercise in respect of hospitals, fire stations, police and army installations and other essential services to the society. In many transition countries, the power to disconnect public sector industries is also largely illusory, since the employment related realities influence the governments to intervene formally or informally. However, it is in Albania that the power company's authority to disconnect even the residential consumers is difficult and dangerous to exercise. As a result of civil disturbances in early 1997 relating to the pyramid schemes, over 700,000 guns are believed to have been stolen from the army depots. Many households still seem to possess these guns and threaten to shoot the power company staff, when they try to detect theft and disconnect supply. Instances of local authorities arresting and imprisoning the power company staff who resort to disconnection are also reported. Improvement of the law and order situation in the country by mopping up the stolen weapons, and dealing with the criminal elements in a manner characterized by understanding and constructive approach with the aim of reintegrating them with civil society based on conflict resolution methodologies are essential prerequisites for all aspects of development, including collection of power bills.

15.   Either on account of shortage of meters or on account other reasons, a good number of consumers seem to receive unmetered supply of electricity from KESH. They are billed on the basis of certain assumptions regarding their monthly consumption. Recent reviews indicate that current assumptions underestimate consumption and that consumption levels for such consumers have to be raised at least by 30%. Such reviews should be undertaken periodically and updated rates notified as frequently as possible[25]. The more important corrective action would be to minimize the number of such unmetered consumers by procuring additional meters and installing them rapidly.

16.   Under financing from Switzerland, computerized loss detection and billing systems have been introduced and are about to become operational in six distribution areas. With consultant assistance these should help in detecting illegal connections by each feeder. Periodic checking and re-calibration of the meters, should help in checking theft by meter tampering. If the proposal to enclose the meters of all apartments in high rise buildings in one place in a locked box and of using co-axial cable connections for the single family homes is found to be cost effective, it should be pursued vigorously. Well known remedies to the problem of theft and poor collection such as: (a) adoption of improved systematic and timely modern public utility practices relating to meter reading, billing and collection; (b) adoption of timely disconnection and reconnection procedures; (c) prosecution of those who steal power; (d) tightening the laws against theft of power and meter tampering, introducing simpler prosecution and summary trial procedures with dedicated mobile courts and prosecutors; (e) pursuing the recovery of unpaid dues through court cases; and (f) writing off the unrecoverable arrears and making provisions in the balance sheet for doubtful debts should all be pursued.

---

[25] Albania law requires parliamentary approval for such revisions. Amending the law to delegate this function to the electricity regulatory authority (ERE) needs to be considered.

17.   More importantly the governments both at the national and local levels should really understand the implications to the economy of power theft and non-payment of bills to the power utility and mobilize public opinion against such practices. The public awareness campaign, which was discontinued prior to the last election should be started again and continued. The key to unlock the problem in Albania seems to be to identify the natural leaders of the opposition groups (who instigated the theft of weapons from the army depots and who foment violence and disturbances) and attempt to integrate them with the mainstream through conflict resolution techniques. The possibility of making use of them as agents for collection and for detecting illegal connections paying them a commission, calculated as a percentage of the resulting savings should be explored. In most countries, when the power company fails to get payments after several notices, it hands over the task to collection agencies, which use a range of legally permissible tactics and collect the dues for commissions ranging from 10% to 40% of amounts collected. This amounts to selling debts at a discount. The fear of the case reaching the collection agencies makes many customers make special efforts to settle the debt. These mechanisms function well in the context of existence of laws to protect property rights, the existence of courts to enforce property rights, the existence of mechanisms to enforce court orders, and the existence of licensed collection agents. In the Albanian context it may be useful to convert the discontented elements into licensed collection agents and private security guards, with vested interest in detecting power theft and collecting power dues. Obviously they could perform similar functions in a range of other sectors, and could grow into a privately owned and useful service industry.

K. Approach to Privatization

18.   Privatizing the distribution function is admittedly the key to overcome payment problems in the long run, when respect for private property takes firm roots in the society, when the state and the courts protect such rights effectively. Privatization of a public sector institution must however result in ownership structures which enable profit maximization, injection of needed additional capital resources and superior management inputs, technology upgrades and increase of labor productivity. The failure of the half hearted attempts made in respect the three small distribution companies highlight the need for a more thoughtful approach in Albania. Care should be taken to ensure: (a) that the resulting privatized distribution entity will have a size enabling economies of scale; and (b) that majority of shares are sold to the strategic partner with relevant experience and qualifications, which can effectively introduce modern utility practices and inject the needed additional capital. It may also be appropriate to alert the strategic partner to the desirability of associating with influential and well connected local entrepreneurs who could provide the local knowledge and linkage to local leadership needed to neutralize the criminal elements in the society. Mass privatization or voucher privatization should be avoided or if at all limited to no more than 10%. Similarly the government owned shares should also be minimal.

19.   Albanian power system is too small to allow a number of generating companies to come into existence and compete with each other meaningfully. Most probably generation and transmission for the whole country should be in one corporatized entity, which should be privatized as a whole, ensuring that majority shares are held by a strategic partner, which can introduce efficient modern public utility management

practices and also provide the needed additional capital. Again significant shareholding by influential local entrepreneurs must also be ensured to successfully neutralize the opposition and violent elements in the society and to make them partners in a profitable and legitimate avocation. When the privatized G&T company and the privatized distribution companies function under regulation by a competent and independent Electricity Regulatory Body (ERE) normal and timely flow of funds from the consumer to the generator(s) could be expected. However, the existence of a strong police and court system, licensed private collection agents and licensed private security guards to enforce property rights would be an essential pre-condition for these companies to succeed. In order to ensure the sustainability of the microeconomic investments financed by the Bank's project loans, the Bank has to focus on the larger issues relating to governance, social development and conflict resolution through adjustment lending and non-lending operations and through more intensive co-operation with IMF and bilateral donors and EBRD.

L. Intermediaries in Distribution Business

20.   From the point of view of cost effectiveness, safety and reliability of power supply, the best practice for a distribution utility is to carry out, directly and by itself, the functions of metering, billing the consumer, and collecting the dues from him. When the utility has to supply power for a large number of contiguously located consumers each with consumption levels too small to be handled directly by the utility, a community association of such consumers could be set up and metered supply provided to such an association, which would have the responsibility to pay for the metered supply. The individual consumers will not have meters and the association will allocate the cost of power equitably among them and collect it from them. Since the association will have a strong interest in continued electricity supply, it is expected to have a better payment performance. Such an association however, can not, afford to have any trained personnel for technical work and therefore all connections and wiring from the association's meter to individual consumers must be done by the utility in accordance with utility standards. Connections to any new member of the association must also be done by the utility and not by the association. These aspects need to be borne in mind while designing power supply facilities to the immigrant settlements near Tirana at Kazma Hill, Lapraka and Bathori under the proposed Urban Land Management Project of the Bank. It is also important to remember that the use of consumer associations did not succeed for long in Armenia. Solutions such as these could only be temporary ones.

21.   However, a word of caution would be appropriate against extending the concept of community associations to cover the so-called electricity re-sellers. Resellers agree to buy power from a metered feeder and resell it to consumers served by the feeder, without any technical organization to handle distribution responsibilities. Experience in many countries have shown that they make service connections of poor quality, create safety problems, overload the feeder in their anxiety to maximize profits, and often resort to black-marketing of power in times of scarcity. In the context of electricity shortage, the Resellers generally have good political connections, become entrenched and difficult to phase out. In most countries resellers have a record of collecting money and not passing it on to the utility, and it becomes problematic to disconnect a large number of paying

56

customers for the fault of the reseller. Creation of Resellers of this type to overcome collection problems must be carefully avoided.

22.   Further, the absence of direct relationship between the utility and the consumer and the absence of signals from the utility regarding the quantum of consumption and cost, would not be conducive to modify the attitude of consumers towards energy conservation and energy use efficiency.

M. Approach to Decentralization

23.   Similarly a word of caution against decentralization of power distribution to the municipalities in Albania would also be in order. Given the overall size of the Albanian power system, such municipal power distribution entities would be too small to have any economy of scale. Also it will make it more difficult to handle non-municipal areas with smaller and scattered loads separately. Given the size of the Albanian power market, the most practical arrangement would be to have not more than two or three distribution entities for the entire country, each having a contiguous mix of urban and rural areas. Most municipalities themselves are financially unsound and frequently default in payments for electricity, and they are even more unlikely to pay for their own consumption when they run the distribution system. Finally, decentralizing water supply, sewerage and district heating to municipalities makes technological sense, as these activities can be discrete and local in character. Power system, on the other hand, is interconnected and its capital intensity calls for economies of scale, not generally available in most small and medium municipal towns, especially in a country with a total population of 3.3 million and a small power system with sales less than 2500 Gwh.

References

1.   Albania- Power Transmission and Distribution Project- SAR, January 1996
2.   Albania- Country Economic Report, July 1994
3.   Albania- Draft Country Assistance Strategy Report, April 1998
4.   Albania- Policy Framework Paper, April 1998
5.   Albania- Household Energy Survey, 1995
6.   Albania- Power Sector Organization Study- Electrowatt-Final Report, 1995
7.   Albania- Information Memorandum on Power Sector, Deloitte Touche and Tohmatsu April 1998
8.   Half- Yearly Progress Reports from KESH
9.   BTORs of Bank staff 1996-1998

THE BULGARIAN CASE STUDY

A. Background

1.   Bulgaria presents an interesting case. Despite serious economic problems faced by it during the 1990s, its non-payment problem, at least in the energy sector, did not reach the alarming proportions it did in many FSU countries, and was brought under control in the course of a few years. This case study attempts to recall the developments in the sector and identify the factors which enabled the government to bring the situation under control.

2.   Bulgaria has a population of about 8.5 million with about 2.9 million households. Its energy resources are modest being limited to some hydro potential in the Aegean and Danube catchment areas and some low quality reserves of lignite and coal. Seventy to seventy-five percent of the country's energy demand is being met by imports. In terms of international trade, it could be regarded as an exposed economy, since its exports and imports have each been in the range of 45% to 60% of its GDP during the last decade.

3.   Following the collapse of the communist regime, GDP declined by a cumulative 30% during the five year period 1989-1993. Unemployment reached a level of 20%. Current account deficits and fiscal deficits reached the level of about 9% of GDP. Inflation which reached a high of 239% in 1991 was in the range of 64% to 96%. By adopting stringent stabilization measures involving tight monetary and fiscal policies, the situation was brought under control and modest growths of 1.8% and 2.0% of GDP were achieved in 1994 and 1995. However the situation turned out to be fragile and the economy experienced a serious crisis in the second half of 1996 and early 1997. GDP fell by 11% and the national currency leva depreciated from 71 leva to 3000 leva to a US dollar. Inflation reached a level of 245% *per month* in February 1997. The Bulgarian National Bank's prime interest rate went up to 180% in December 1996 and to 216% in March 1997. Foreign exchange reserves went down to a level equivalent to one month's import. The government tackled the situation by undertaking structural reforms, in the fiscal, banking and enterprise sectors, by pegging leva to DM and adopting a Currency Board Agreement. By early 1998, inflation came down to 1% to 2% per month, fiscal deficit came down to 2.6% of GDP and exchange reserves rose to the level of 6 month's imports. Interest rates[26] currently are around 7% p.a. and GDP growth of about 4% for 1998 is anticipated. Unlike in the case some FSU countries, after the collapse of the communist regime Bulgaria did not experience any major political upheaval or civil unrest. It suffered however from unstable governments on account of changing political alliances.

B. Electric Power Sector

4.   Electricity generation declined from the level of 49.2 Twh in 1988 to 41.0 Twh in 1991 and the level 35.6 Twh in 1992 and recovered to the level of 42.8 Twh in 1996.

---

[26] The Bulgarian National Bank's prime interest rate as of 5 June 1998 was 5.12% and the exchange rate for lev was $1 = 1771.6 leva.

Data relating to generation, imports , exports and domestic sales and consumption of electricity are summarized below:

Item	1992	1993	1994	1995	1996
Generation (Gwh)	35569	37902	38176	42003	42801
Imports (Gwh)	3289	1634	1173	1961	1803
Exports (Gwh)	584	1518	1245	2121	2252
Generation + Net Imports (Gwh)	38274	38018	38104	41843	42352
Total System Losses (Gwh)[27]	10939	10978	10932	11809	12039
Domestic Sales (Gwh)	27335	27040	27172	30034	30313
Share of Industry in Sales (%)	53.2	50.9	51.9	51.6	50.4
Share of Households in Sales (%)	35.3	37.1	36.1	36.5	37.9

Source: WB Internal Documents

The share of industry in electricity consumption went down from 56.5% in 1988 to about 50% during 1992-96. The share of households increased from 25.2% in 1988 to about 38% in 1996. By and large the shift in the relative shares of industry and households is not as pronounced in Bulgaria as in many FSU countries. It may even have been overstated somewhat because of the different classification used for 1988 and the period 1992-96.

5.   Bulgaria had an installed power generating capacity of 12, 074 MW in 1991. The composition of this capacity and the energy generated in 1991 is given in the table below:

Item	Capacity MW	Energy Generated Gwh
Hydro	1970	2411
Thermal	6344	23209
Nuclear	3760	13184
Total	12074	38834

Source: WB Internal Documents

The availability of the lignite fired thermal plants was low and forced outages were frequent. By 1992 the available thermal capacity was only 4730 MW nearly 75% of that available a year earlier. By the end of 1996 available thermal capacity increased to 4950 MW and two new units at the Chaira Pumped storage Project was added raising the hydro capacity to 2407 MW. In addition industrial units had captive power generating capacity of 842 MW and the District Heating companies had a capacity of 758 MW. NEK purchased from them and from small privately owned hydropower units a total of 1523.7 Gwh of energy in 1996. The system peak demand in winter 1996 was slightly lower than 8000 MW and that during summer was slightly higher than 4000 MW.

6.   In response to the economic downturn in 1990 and 1991, the government liberalized most prices (except those of energy), demonopolized industry and trade, introduced two tier banking, enacted a company law, and converted the state enterprises into joint stock companies to enable their eventual privatization. Before 1991, lignite and coal mines, power and heat enterprises were all together under the Committee on Energy and transactions among them was regarded as internal. In November 1991, National

---

[27] This includes self consumption in generating plants, transmission and distribution losses and commercial losses. At around 28% to 29%, the level is considered high and should be the focus of further efforts.

Electric Company (NEK) was formed as a joint stock company to handle the responsibility for power generation, transmission and distribution as a vertically integrated utility. Separate companies for heat supply and coal mines were formed and transactions among them and NEK became inter-company transactions. NEK was organized with 11 branches for generation, 28 branches for power distribution, 2 branches for investment and one for servicing of hydro power stations, besides its Head Office (including the National Dispatch Center).[28] These branches had considerable autonomy of operations. The National Dispatch Center includes 4 Regional Dispatch centers and 28 District Dispatch Centers -all equipped with SCADA systems. High voltage transmission was by 750 kV, 400 kV, 220 kV, and 110 kV; medium voltage lines included 20 kV, 10kV, and 6.3 kV; while the low voltage lines were 380/220 kv.

C. The Emergence of the Payment Problem

7.   In order to catch up with inflation at least partially, power prices were increased 12 fold during 1990-92. Average tariff per kWh rose from 0.0524 lev in 1990 to 0.57 lev in May 1992 and to 0.64 lev in January 1993. Though the tariff structure improved somewhat, households continued to be heavily subsidized. Heat prices for industry increased 19 fold and that for household increased 11 fold. Still the average tariff at 260 leva /G.Cal was only 60% of the cost of supply.

8.   The increase in tariffs combined with decline in GDP and adverse macroeconomic factors such as high inflation, interest rates, fiscal deficits and tight money policy resulted in the poor profitability of Bulgarian firms and their cash flows deteriorated sharply, when their working capital needs became greater. This resulted in a rapid growth of inter-company debts. As it happened, NEK was a net beneficiary, as it was a net recipient 3.6 billion leva credit from the coal mines and power exporters to Bulgaria. Still NEK was defaulting on its tax dues to the government. The 1992 balance sheet of NEK showed an accounts receivable of 4.114 billion leva (**3.04 months sales equivalent**) and an accounts payable of 7.674 billion leva (5.64 months sales equivalent). NEK continued to have difficulty in collecting its dues and the accounts receivable rose to 5.4 billion leva (**2.4 months sales equivalent**) at the end of 1993. More than 45% of the dues were from state owned enterprises (SOEs). NEK's own payable rose to 3.4 billion leva at the end of 1993 and to 6.0 billion leva at the end of 1994.

---

[28] Some consolidation has taken place since. Currently NEK has, besides its head office(including NDC), only 28 branches--10 for generation, 15 for transmission and distribution, 2 for investment and one for hydro maintenance

D. Return to Normalcy

9.   During the period 1994-1997, the situation improved a great deal, notwithstanding a major economic crisis faced by the country during later half of 1996 and early 1997. For the year 1997, NEK turned in a profit[29] and at the end of the year had an accounts receivable level **equivalent to 36 days of sales**-- which is considered a remarkable achievement. This turnaround was achieved by a combination of the Utility's determined efforts to collect its dues, government's willingness to respond to the Bank's persuasive advice to adjust tariffs to ensure financial viability of NEK and to deal effectively with the problem of loss making SOEs, and the cooperation of the parliament to enact enabling laws.

E. Disconnection Policies

10.   NEK was successful in persuading the parliament to pass a law enabling disconnection of supplies to customers who defaulted in payment of their dues. The law provided that power supply would not be cut off arbitrarily, but enabled disconnection after due notice and for good cause (such as default in payment of legitimate dues, theft of power, etc.). The utility used this power extensively in respect of residential customers, resisted successfully and tactfully interference by individual politicians, and ensured that residential customers paid their dues on time. The threat of disconnection was also used effectively in respect of large industries. The country's largest steel mill was disconnected for non-payment, and it went to court against this action. Using the threat of non- supply during the pendency of the suit, the company was persuaded to settle the case out of court. The court system and the laws relating to property rights were reasonable and enabled the utility to obtain favorable decisions in similar cases, though the court proceedings were characterized by delays.

F. Working with the Customers

11.   Having established disconnection as a credible threat, the utility proceeded to work systematically with its largest customers to improve their businesses, using its own standing in the commercial and credit markets. NEK's management evolved a company policy of strategic attention to its largest customers to reduce the level of arrears from them. The CEO shouldered a major responsibility in this regard, and allocated to each of the top executives a specific region in the country to focus on. NEK understood clearly that it is not by merely cutting off major customers that a power company becomes viable. A list of top 30 of its largest customers was made and the senior executives of NEK worked with each of them to improve customers' cash flows and to collect the arrears. Krassimir Kanev, one of former top executives of NEK recalls how he helped a customer to market his surplus stock of cigarettes in Russia, and another to obtain an

---

[29] Based on Bulgarian accounting practices, NEK made a profit of $ 193 million in 1997. When translated as per IAS practices, making provisions for the decommissioning of the nuclear plant, doubtful debts, and depreciation as per IAS, the company would appear to have made a post tax loss of $ 113 million as per the draft audited statements of 1997 (Compare this with the net fixed assets of NEK valued at $ 3.773 billion and annual sales of $ 895 million). The pre-tax profit however was $ 126 million, even as per audit statement.

attractive export contract in Spain using NEK's contacts, influence and credit rating, so that these customers could settle their debts to NEK from the proceeds of such transactions.

12.   Two other examples are worth mentioning. A large fertilizer plant, which claimed that electricity supplies to it should not be cut for technological (non-interruptible chemical process), safety and environmental (potential for explosion and deadly emissions) reasons and continued to default on its payments to the electricity supplier (NEK) despite several attempts by NEK to restructure the debt and collect the dues. Ultimately NEK gave the fertilizer factory a written notice of disconnection several weeks in advance of the proposed date of disconnection to enable the factory to shut down without major production losses and without endangering environment, and remained firm in its resolve not to resume supply till credible arrangements could be made to clear the arrears. Simultaneously NEK persuaded the sales chain of one of its suppliers to export the output of the fertilizer factory. The proceeds of the export sales were to be remitted into an escrow account from which 30% would go to meet the operational expenses of the fertilizer factory, another 30% would go to service the restructured debt to NEK and the remaining 40% would go to meet the costs of current electricity consumption to ensure that no new arrears were accumulated. Electricity supply was resumed on the basis of these arrangements, which proved effective in solving a long standing problem. Similar constructive action was taken in respect of the steel mill mentioned earlier in paragraph 10. NEK used its connections and contacts to arrange for the export of steel and had the proceeds from export sales assigned to it as collateral. From these proceeds it retained 65% for servicing the restructured debt (to NEK)and for the current electricity consumption of the steel mill. The remaining 35% of the proceeds was transferred to the steel mill to finance its operations. This philosophy of working with major customers appears to have paid rich dividends in the Bulgarian context.

G. Government Approach to Loss Making SOEs

13.   The government's approach to the elimination of the problem of loss making SOEs was noteworthy, in this context. As early as in 1991, the government ordered the break up of large "Kombinats" into separate enterprises and exposed them to international competition, and effectively eliminated cross subsidies among them. To enable eventual privatization all SOEs were corporatized. Losses from SOEs amounted to 27% of the GDP in 1993, came down to 12% in 1995, but rose again to 19% in 1996. About 130 SOEs accounted for more than 92% of the total losses. Dishonest practices of buying inputs at high prices and selling outputs at low prices engaging intermediaries to enable private sector profit and public sector loss was widely practiced by the managers of these units. By end 1996, the total debts of SOEs amounted to 750 billion leva or 44% of the GDP. Of these, debts to suppliers amounted to 55.2%, followed by debts to the Budget (24.7%), Banks (14.6%), and employees (5.5%).

14.   During 1996, the government identified 64 loss making units (which accounted for 28% of the total SOE losses) for immediate liquidation. Within a year the government liquidated 59 of these large units and 86 smaller ones and achieved the target of reducing losses by 28%. Next 71 large loss making units including 30 utilities and some mines

(Group A) and 41 SOEs in the competitive sector (Group B) were put in an "isolation program". Together they accounted for 50% of the SOE losses. The "isolated" enterprises were isolated from further bank financing, made to face hard budget constraints, were granted a moratorium on debts, asked to prepare a financial recovery plan and conclude conciliation agreements with their creditors. Group A enterprises were allowed to increase their tariffs, required to cut their costs and achieve a level of cash flow adequate to cover operational expenses and financial charges at the end of isolation. Meanwhile their operational losses were met from the state budget in a transparent manner through explicit line items. Group B companies were to be liquidated, if they could not be privatized. This program was also successfully completed in 1997.

15.   The 30 utilities in Group A increased their tariffs, cut their costs and collected their dues much better especially in the context of a cabinet resolution requiring the utilities to disconnect service and demand advance payment from SOEs in arrears exceeding 30 days. The government also set up a high level monitoring system to review arrears reports on a weekly basis to enable timely punitive or corrective action. The government has firmly declared its intention to ensure that aggregate payment arrears to utilities will not be allowed to increase from the level at the end of June 1997.

16.   Privatization of loss making SOEs was pursued through restitution, cash sales and mass privatization. The progress had been slow till two or three years ago and in the last two years the privatization is being accelerated.

H. Approach to Budget Entities

17.   In respect of entities financed from the state budget, such as the army, the hospitals, and schools, Parliament was persuaded to provide for specific line item budgets for their energy payment needs. The budget law further enabled these amounts to be set off against dues from NEK to the government. By following this mechanism, the need to threaten them with disconnection was dispensed with.

I. Tariffs and Social Protection of the Poor

18.   Another key aspect of the successful approach towards the payment problem in Bulgaria was the acceptance by the government of the idea (though slowly and gradually) that tariffs had to be set at a level enabling the financial viability of the utility and approach the LRMC of supply to achieve economic efficiency in the context of monopolistic supply of electricity, while protecting the poorer sections of the population from the resulting increased tariff by giving them direct social relief, without distorting the structure of power tariff. Such an approach nipped in the bud, a possible payment problem from residential consumers, while serving the economic efficiency and utility viability criteria. Thus with the active assistance from World Bank, the utility demonstrated to the government: (a) that the electricity prices had only a small weight in the general price index and that the effects of an electricity price increase on inflation would be more than off set by increased tax payments by NEK and the reduction in deficit financing by both NEK and the government, which was the major contributor to inflation; and (b) that the electricity expenses were only 2.6% of the average household expenditures, and that even with the proposed price increases, the electricity price would

rise slower than wages. Even a 50% increase in power prices would only increase the CPI by 1.25%, whereas the financial burden of keeping the power prices low would be as high as 1.5% of the GDP. Keeping the overall prices low did not help the poor. Since the formula follows the rule, "the higher the consumption, the higher the subsidy", wealthiest 10% of the households got 67% more subsidy than the poorest 10%.

19.   Thus the government revised the power tariffs and heat tariffs several times and (in local currency terms) several fold. Since May 1996, the tariffs are also adjusted monthly for changes in inflation rates and foreign exchange rates of lev. The average price per kWh rose from 0.0524 lev in 1990 to 57.85 leva in May 1998 (US cents 3.25) without VAT. The price with VAT amounted to 70.31 leva or US cents 3.95. This compares with the supply cost of about US cents 2.6 and an LRMC range of US cents 3.77 to 4.06 per kWh. The average tariff per kWh for households in May 1998 was US cents 2.91 and that for industries was US cents 4.56. Thus while the overall tariff was close to LRMC, internal cross subsidization of households by industrial customers still lingers on, and is area for future correction.

20.   The average heat price per G.cal for house holds in May 1998 was $ 14 without VAT and $ 17 with VAT. This compares with the supply cost at $ 23.24 without VAT. The cost of heating a small apartment amounts to $ 36 per month, which compares with the pension range of $ 28 to $ 56 per month in Bulgaria.

21.   The government introduced a means tested voucher system, based on the income and the size of the house, enabling those with an income of up to 150% of a nationally defined basic minimum income to get graduated subsidy in the form of energy vouchers direct from the government to pay for their coal, heat and electricity bills. The households could use the vouchers to pay fully or partially their energy bills and the energy companies could cash the vouchers from the Government.[30] This   arrangement is estimated to cover about 10 to 11 % of the total households in the country. VAT is not applicable to electricity sold to household consumers. When prices are raised to the level of marginal costs, the resulting increased VAT collections from the sale of electricity to customers other than households is believed to be adequate to meet the cost of this social support to the poorer sections of the society. The efficacy and sustainability of this arrangement are yet to be fully evaluated. Nonetheless an approach like this has clearly enabled the government to fight successfully the payment problem, utility viability problem and the economic efficiency problem, which are intricately inter-linked.

J. Why did Bulgaria Succeed?

22.   Why did Bulgaria succeed in taming the payment problem, despite the serious economic debacles it faced during 1992-93 and then again in 1996-97? What lessons can we learn from this case? In the absence of further data collection and analysis the answers could only be intuitive and conjectural. First, Bulgaria is a unitary state and NEK did not have to contend with the problem of federal-regional political tensions, as in the case of

---

[30] According to the present Finance Director of NEK, the company did not face any difficulty in cashing the vouchers from the government.

Russia or Ukraine. Second, while Bulgaria suffered from unstable governments caused by shifting political alignments, it did not experience any major upheaval or war or serious civil strife as in the case of some FSU states. Third, the society and economy was not criminalized and was not dominated by any entrenched Mafia or oligarchs and no one got rich quickly without every one noticing it. Fourth, because of its exposure to the west through IMF, World Bank, and other similar international organizations, and its trade links, it was more receptive to the practices of market economies and had a head start in the building up of the legal infrastructure needed for market economies. Thus its new Constitution (1991), Commercial Code, Competition Law, Restitution Laws(1991), Privatization Law(1992), Bankruptcy Law (1994), Banking Law, and Prudential Regulations of the Central Bank, VAT Law (1993), Foreign Investment Law and similar laws gave the country "solid general legal framework for a market economy." They enabled a clear recognition of property rights and effective mechanisms including a working judicial system to enforce them. Fifth, while NEK was not privatized or unbundled, its corporate governance was obviously adequate to mobilize political support for favorable disconnection policies and tariff adjustments and other forms of Government support to overcome the payment and viability problems. The politicians, though often tempted to interfere and meddle, happened to be enlightened enough to back off when national interests and conformity with the law became an issue. Parliaments, despite their political bickering, by and large, delivered on legislation needed for reform. Finally, being basically an exposed economy (in trade parlance), Bulgaria is accustomed to a fully monetized cash economy, and never developed an appetite for barter deals, vexels and questionable instruments of that kind, and has a tax system and structure which, unlike in the case of FSU states, do not discriminate against cash transactions.

K. What do we learn from this case?

23.   The key lesson we learn from the Bulgarian case is that reasonable corporate governance and determined leadership of the utility and its stress on doing its job well could deliver results, despite the utility being vertically integrated or state owned, and despite serious unfavorable economic environment. Another key lesson is that at the utility level, attention paid by top executives to build mutually beneficial customer relations with top consumers, and work with them to improve their businesses, yields rich dividends to the utility in the long run. The constant and continuous focus of the Bank staff, on adjustment of tariffs to approach marginal cost levels and to protect the poor through targeted social assistance and the strategy of strengthening the hands of the utility in dealing with the government for achieving these objectives are noteworthy examples of best practice within the Bank.

REFERENCES

1.   Bulgaria Energy Project – SAR, February 1993
2.   Bulgaria Power Demand and Supply Options Study, June 1993
3.   A Strategy for Electric Power and Nuclear Safety, May 1994
4.   Bulgaria- Electricity Pricing: Economic and Social Issues, July 1995
5.   Bulgaria- Country Assistance Strategy, March 1996
6.   Bulgaria- Country Assistance Strategy, April 1998

7.   Bulgaria- Private Sector Assessment, June 1996
8.   Financial & Enterprises Sector Adjustment Loan-
          President's Report, October 1997
9.   BTORs of Bank Staff, 1995-1998
10.   Interview with Krassimir Kanev, a former top executive of NEK in August 1998
11.   Annual Reports of NEK, 1993 to 1996
12.   Draft Audit Report of NEK,s financial statements for 1997

THE HUNGARIAN CASE STUDY

A. Background

1.   Hungary is one of the few countries in the ECA region which did not experience any major or sustained non-payment problem in the energy sector, even though like other east European countries, it too experienced major economic upheavals during its transition to market economy. This case study attempts to identify the policies followed by Hungary, which enabled it to avoid serious non-payment problems.

2.   Hungary is an upper middle income country with an estimated per capita GNP of $4530 (1997) and a population of 10.6 million. It has notable reserves of hard coal, brown coal and lignite and modest reserves of uranium, oil and natural gas. Overall its import dependency for its energy needs is about 50%, which is likely to increase owing to the rapid depletion of its domestic reserves.

B. Power Sector: Dimensions, Organizations and Structure

3.   Its installed power generation capacity is about 7350 MW consisting of a nuclear plant (1840 MW), several coal, oil or gas fired steam turbines (4968 MW), gas turbines (494 MW) and hydroelectric plants (48 MW). Taking into account the de-rating of the units and also some imported power, the total available capacity was 7427 MW compared to the peak demand of 5850 MW in 1996 providing a comfortable reserve margin of about 27%. The system reliability is considered high and system losses (auxiliary consumption at 8% and Transmission and distribution losses at 12%) are considered acceptable.

4.   Out of the total consumption of 29.0 Twh[31] in 1995, the share of the industrial consumers was 40% followed by households (33.8%) and others (26.2%). A decade earlier in 1984, the share of industrial consumers was 50% and that of households was 23%. As a result of the contraction of GDP during 1989-1994, the share of industrial consumption has declined. The 1989 level of consumption (40.7 Twh) is expected to be reached by the year 2003.

5.   Till 1991 all the power facilities were being operated by MVM Trust which was a vertically integrated power utility owned by the state. It had centralized management control over the entire power system comprising 11 generating units, the transmission system, the national (1) and regional (6) load dispatch centers, six distribution systems, 30 distribution control centers and four supporting service units. In 1992, the sector was reorganized and MVM Trust has become a holding company (MVM Rt) with 15 subsidiary companies one each for the nuclear plant, seven conventional generating plants, the transmission and load dispatch system, and six power distribution systems. MVM Rt itself is fully owned by the state. It owns fully the nuclear plant and the transmission and load dispatching system. During 1995-98 all six distribution systems

---

[31] Twh equals one billion kWh

and all generating units (except the nuclear plant) have been privatized by selling about 49% of the shares to strategic investors. MVM Rt which owns the transmission grid buys power from the generating companies on the basis of long term power purchase contracts , transmits and sells to the distribution companies on the basis of long term power sales contracts. The sector is regulated by Hungarian Energy Office, which reports to the Minister of Industry and Trade and to the Prime Minister. MVM Rt buys power at different prices from the different generating companies, pools the power and sells it at a uniform price to all power distribution companies, which in turn sell power to the end users on the basis of tariffs which are uniform all over the country. HEO recommends, and the cabinet approves tariffs, based on a rate of return criterion of 8% on equity, incorporating efficiency norms and a price cap formula. These arrangements are subject to review in 2001.

C. The Accounts Receivable Level in the Power Sector

6.   Based on a review of the staff appraisal reports prepared during the period 1986-1997, and other related documentation available in the Bank, it is seen that the account receivable situation in MVM Trust (later MVM Rt) had been well under control through out the period. The accounts receivable expressed in equivalent months of billing or sales has ranged from 0.45 months to 1.79 months. During the period 1992- 1995, when the economy was facing upheavals and was recovering from them, the level ranged from 1.62 months to 1.79 months. MVM Trust as the transmission grid company was adopting daily settlements of accounts with the generating and distributing subsidiaries; from its accounts receivable position it is possible to infer that the distribution companies did not face major payment problems.

Table 1: Accounts Receivable Situation in MVM Trust/ MVM Rt.
(Amounts in HUF billion)

Year	Annual Sales Revenue	Accounts Receivable (AR)	AR in Equivalent Months of Sales
1988	99.7	3.7	0.45
1989	104.1	6.2	0.71
1990	123.4	9.2	0.89
1991	160.5	10.4	0.77
1992	159.7	23.8	1.79
1993	101.4	13.7	1.62
1994	99.5	14.4	1.73
1995	123.7	17.0	1.64
1996	170.3	7.4	0.52
1997	209.9	8.0	0.45

Source: WB Internal Documents

The six distribution companies together had a total accounts receivable of HUF 5.0 billion at the time of their privatization and the government decided that the buyers of these companies must assume the associated commercial risk. As a percentage of the annual sales of the distribution companies the level of the accounts receivable was insignificant.

D. The Hungarian Situation

7.   Basically Hungary's quest for economic reforms commenced as early as 1968, when rigid central planning gradually gave way to reliance on indirect "economic regulators" such as taxes, subsidies, wage and price controls, and licensing to influence demand and the direction of the economy. It was also operating an exposed economy in which imports and exports were equivalent to about 80% of the GDP. Towards the end of the 1980s and early 1990s, when the centrally planned economies collapsed in east Europe, Hungary had already in place a two tier banking system (central bank and commercial banks), a company law and a legal framework for entry and exit of investments and specific laws enabling bankruptcy and liquidation of enterprises, a tax system based on income of individuals and profits of enterprises and value added, a substantially liberalized price regime and a small but notable number of private enterprises. It was a member of the IMF, the Bank and was later admitted to the membership of GATT and in 1992 to the membership of OECD. Its exposure to market economies was thus greater than the other socialist economies.

8.   During the economic turmoil faced by all the east European countries, Hungary experienced a contraction of its GDP by 17% during 1989-1993, a moderate revival of growth at 1.5 to 2% during 1994-96, and a steadier growth of 4% or more thereafter. It experienced severe fiscal deficits and current account deficits (of about 9% of GDP in 1994) and had to manage serious foreign exchange and inflation problems. As a result of reforms since 1995, the fiscal deficit was brought down to about 3.1 % of GDP. The current account deficit came down to about 3.3% of GDP. Ratio of external debt to GDP came down from 45% to 30%. The privatization program including those of banks, was virtually completed by end 1997. The country obtained investment grade rating towards the end of 1997 and external borrowing became available at interest rates 35 basis points above LIBOR-- representing a drop of 200 basis point from previous levels. Accession to EU is expected within a few years.

E. Approach to Energy Pricing

9.   Its administered price regimes had been in place for over 15 years and energy prices had been periodically adjusted in response to external fuel price changes, since its economy was import dependent for energy. Thus when the economic systems of the former energy suppliers collapsed and energy imports had to be paid for at world prices, the price shock was somewhat less in Hungary than in other countries and it had a mechanism to adjust prices from time to time. Through periodic price adjustments the rate of growth of energy consumption was brought down from 37% during 1970-75 to 17% during 1975-80 and 6% during 1980-85. Elasticity of energy demand with reference to GDP growth which was above 1.0 in 1970s came down to 0.46 in 1985-87. By 1989, prices of oil products in Hungary were at or higher than world prices. Electricity prices for the productive sector were close to LRMC., though the prices for households lagged behind costs of supply.

10.   In the wake of the country having to pay world market prices for energy imports, the government in 1991 freed petroleum products from price controls, reduced import duties on them and allowed freely their imports. During 1991-92, subsidy to the

households from the government budget for energy was virtually eliminated by raising the regulated energy prices substantially. In 1992 price controls over LPG, fuel wood and coal were removed and the authority to regulate the end user tariff for district heating was decentralized to the municipalities, which owned the district heating systems. It was estimated that the price revisions in 1992 for the supply of power and natural gas to the households resulted in price levels equivalent to 70% and 80% of the economic costs respectively.[32] During 1991-96, power tariffs went up in nominal terms by 160 -200 %, though in US dollar terms the increase was only 20-30%. In the wake of sector reorganization, the government formally recognized that tariffs for the generation, transmission and distribution entities should enable full cost recovery including depreciation on revalued assets, environment related costs, insurance, interest, land reclamation, decommissioning of nuclear plant and a 8% return on the equity employed for energy operations. As of January 1998, MVM Rt was purchasing electricity from the various privatized generators at an average price / kWh of US cents 3.40 (the prices ranged from US cents 2.06 to 8.76). MVM Rt was selling power to the distributing utilities at a wholesale price / kWh of US cents 3.65. The average retail price charged by the distribution utilities to the end users was US cents 5.83 / kWh. The charges for households stood at US cents 6.25 / kWh (without VAT) or 11.5% higher than the charge for non-residential consumers at US cents 5.60 / kWh. Though, often slow and somewhat late, the process of tariff revisions had been effective in sensitizing the consumers to increasing supply costs and shielding them from sudden price shocks, as was the case in many other socialist economies.

F. Causes for the Accumulation of Inter-Enterprise Arrears

11.   In the second half of 1980s the government undertook a set of reforms involving greater decentralization of public enterprise management, freedom for them to set wages to attract talent and promote labor mobility and also freedom for them to set the price of their products. In the context of somewhat lax fiscal policy and the inertia in closing down insolvent public enterprises, these reforms led to the perverse results of the insolvent enterprises increasing the wages of their personnel and trying to pass the costs on to the consumer using their new found freedom to set prices. In this environment when the authorities adopted a tight money policy to overcome current account deficit problems, a problem of substantial inter-enterprise arrears emerged, as the insolvent firms forced other enterprises to finance large accounts receivable. Total arrears to other enterprises and the banks (excluding payment arrears of less than HUF 25 million) amounted to HUF 73 billion or 4.3% of GDP by end 1989. More than 300 enterprises were involved. About half the arrears were from engineering and light industry sub-sectors which had lost export sales to CEMA countries. Metallurgy sector and trade sector accounted for 10% and 16% of the arrears respectively. Though the danger from this behavior did not affect the energy entities significantly, the parliament enacted a law enabling the energy entities to disconnect supplies to defaulting public enterprises. Application of this procedure to the steel industry resulted in huge demonstrations by over 30,000 workers and the government realized that what is involved is not merely the adoption of a good business practice, but a much deeper sociopolitical problem.

---

[32] Except in the case of households covered by life line tariffs.

70

G. Collection from Households

12.   By and large non-payment for the power dues was not a major problem with households despite a series of revision of power tariffs. Several reasons are attributed for this. First the distribution companies had traditionally adopted good and systematic procedures for metering, billing and collection and there were no inhibitions to adopt the disconnection procedure in respect of defaulting customers. Second, legislation approved in 1990 enabled disconnection of power supply to those who defaulted in payments, though it provided for adequate notices and a due process and a moratorium of 90 days for the outstanding debt. Third, Hungarians as a class preferred to pay their bills and were culturally averse to accumulating personal debts. Fourth, the preferential tariffs for households were widely exploited by small and cottage industries, artisans and small commercial entrepreneurs (whose emergence) was notable during this period) who chose to set up shop using households as a front. They always paid their bills promptly to avoid any inspection and ensuing complications. Fifth, under the various IMF programs and the adjustment loans of the Bank, the government was continuously refining its social safety-net arrangements to protect the poorer sections which were less than 10% of the population. In 1997 the government set up a social Compensation Fund of HUF 1.5 billion with contributions of HUF 1.0 billion from its tax revenues and HUF 0.5 billion from the somewhat reluctant newly privatized distribution companies and MVM Rt. In 1998 the size of the fund is HUF 800 million contributed equally by the government and the companies mentioned above. This fund is for compensating annually about 380,000 vulnerable households for their additional electricity related expenses to the extent of about HUF 1700 to 12000 per household. A similar fund has been created for natural gas sector also. These arrangements are considered temporary till the year 2000, when life line rates would be adopted with a different kind of funding arrangement by the government. Such social protection arrangements helped to minimize arrears from the household sector.

H. Government's Approach to the Problem of State Enterprises

13.   In the case of state owned enterprises, which became insolvent on account of the contraction of GDP and loss of domestic and export markets, the government adopted different approaches at different stages. In retrospect they could be summarized as consisting of: (a) opening the economy to private sector, promoting small and medium industrial and commercial ventures, and attracting foreign direct investment, *inter alia*, as a means of creating new employment[33]; (b) exposing the domestic industry to international competition through liberalization of the trade regimes and removing tariff and non-tariff barriers to imports; (c) phased elimination of price controls and restrictions on domestic trade, as well as freeing the entry of any enterprise into the export trade; (d) phased elimination of producer and consumer subsidies from the state budget[34]; (e) granting operational autonomy to the enterprises including freedom to determine wages

---

[33] The number of employees permitted in private business was increased from 30 to 500 in 1988. This employment limit was abolished in 1990.

[34] These came down from the level of 13% of GDP in 1989 to 4% in 1993.

for its employees and the prices of its outputs; (f) enactment of bankruptcy and liquidation laws, which based on several amendments became "the best and most modern among those legislated in the former socialist economies"; (g) enforcement of the liquidation of insolvent firms through the banks, when they were arrears to the banks and by the tax authorities when they were in default of tax payments and enforcing bankruptcy procedures when the commercial bills of exchange of enterprises could no longer be eligible for rediscounting by their commercial banks at the central bank; (h) enacting the law of transformation under which the state enterprises were converted into joint stock companies, enabling their privatization through sale of shares; (i) enactment of the new accounting law which made the accounting system in Hungary conform to IAS and GAAP and standard disclosure norms as well as the adoption of external audits based on these; (j) rationalizing the taxation laws, reducing the corporate tax rates and reforming the VAT structure; (k) enactment of the Security Market Law to provide the framework for orderly trading of securities, establishing the deregulation board and the office of competition to eliminate regulations encumbering free markets and promoting competition; and (l) privatizing a majority of state owned enterprises and all the commercial banks adopting the method of selling controlling shares to carefully and transparently selected strategic investors.

I. The Sequencing of Reforms

14. The key sequencing was to create conditions for new employment creation and thereafter force the pace of restructuring, privatization and liquidation (all resulting in loss of jobs) to minimize the trauma of transition. Foreign investors were given unrestricted freedom to repatriate their dividends and their invested capital and the emerging economic and legal framework in the country enabled to attract the highest level of foreign investment among all former socialist countries. Thus foreign direct investment in 1995 amounted to $ 4.4 billion or 10.1% of GDP. By 1989-90 over 9000 new companies came into existence through privatization of profitable state assets. Between 1990 and 1994, private capital in incorporated enterprises grew by HUF 1.5 trillion of which two thirds was by new investment and one third by acquisition of state assets. FDI accounted for 50% of the private investment. Taking into account the formal and informal segments[35], the share of the private sector was over 60% of GDP by the end of 1994. The formal sector accounted for 50% of the GDP and 50% of the employment.

15. An environment like this made it possible to restructure state owned enterprises in the difficult sectors of coal and ferrous metallurgical industries, involving significant loss of jobs. The process of downsizing of coal industry started in 1989 and by 1997 thirteen out of twenty-seven mines were closed, output from underground mines were reduced by about 5 million tons per year and the number of employees reduced from 50,000 to 21, 000. The mines with acceptable production costs were integrated with the power generating companies to which they supplied coal and were privatized. Only five remaining coal mines with 10% of the total out put remain outside such integration and

---

[35] Formally incorporated entities exceeded 100,000 in number. The informal segment comprised 120,000 unincorporated entities and 780,000 individual entrepreneurs.

these are scheduled for closure by the end of 1998. Ferrous metallurgical industries were also restructured in phases.

J. Banking Reforms

16.   Subsequent key phases related to the reforms of the banking sector and aggressive privatization of the remaining enterprises through sales to strategic investors. The commercial banks continued to finance the insolvent state owned enterprises in the early nineties resulting in the inter- enterprise arrears problem becoming one of arrears to the banking system and accumulation of non-performing assets. The government tightened the law relating to bankruptcy, requiring enterprises with outstanding arrears of more than 90 days to automatically file for bankruptcy[36]. The government also forced the banks to review the financial condition of their clients and identify those to be liquidated. Action pursued in respect 42 enterprises led to 12 of them repaying the debt or submitting acceptable restructuring plans and the remaining 30 (with arrears totaling HUF 4.2 billion and with an employment of 20,000 persons) being liquidated. Similar action was pursued in respect of 453 enterprises in 1990 with assets exceeding HUF 165 billion and employees exceeding 141,000. Banking laws were amended requiring the banks to adopt Basle conventions regarding capital adequacy, provision for bad debts and treatment of non-performing assets and prudential regulatory framework. The government also undertook to recapitalize the banks extensively and in the final phase(1995-97) privatized the banks by selling controlling shares to strategic investors who were mostly reputed foreign banks.

K. Privatization to Strategic Investors

17.   During the period 1995-97, government came to the conclusion that in order to bring in and sustain good management, the state enterprises have to be privatized adopting the method of selling controlling interest to strategic foreign investors and proceeded to amend the laws relating privatization, revamp the organizations charged with the responsibility of undertaking the privatization process and carried out the sale of shares adopting a transparent tendering and decision making process. The privatization program of the state enterprises is believed to have been virtually completed in this manner by the end of 1997. In the power sector proposals are under consideration to privatize MVM Rt (which owns the grid and the nuclear plant) with government retaining 50% plus one share. Most of the other energy sector entities oil, power and gas have been privatized.

18.   Energy sector in Hungary had been the beneficiary of the various reform efforts of the government, which brought in financial discipline to nip the emerging problem of non-payments in the bud. The success of the government's privatization program has ensured the continued healthy functioning of the energy entities.

---

[36] During 1992-93 there were 5000 filings for bankruptcy by managers and 16,000 filings for liquidation by creditors.

REFERENCES

1. President's Report and recommendations SAL I, May 1990
2. President's Report and Recommendations SAL II, May 1991
3. Hungary Reform and Decentralization of the Public Sector, May 1992
4. Project Completion Report : Hungary SAL I, April 1993
5. Hungary: Structural Reforms for Sustainable Growth, June 1995
6. Energy Policies of Hungary: 1995 Survey, IEA/OECD, 1995
7. Implementation Completion Report: Hungary SAL II, November 1996
8. President's Report and Recommendations and Technical Annex: Hungary Public Finance Management Project, November 1996
9. President's Report and Recommendations: Hungary Enterprise and Financial Sector Adjustment Loan, February 1997
10. SAR of Hungary: Quick Start Gas Turbine Project, March 1997
11. Central and Eastern Europe: Power Sector Reform in Selected Countries, ESMAP Report No.196/97, July 1997
12. Hungary: Country Assistance Strategy, December 1997
13. SAR Hungary: Energy Development and Conservation Project, April 1989
14. SAR Hungary: Power Project, April 1986
15. SAR Hungary: Energy and Environment Project, January 1994
16. BTOR of Bank staff dated March 17, 1998

THE ARMENIAN CASE STUDY

A. Background

1.   Armenia, a land-locked country with a population of 3.7 million, became independent in September 1991. It had already experienced a major earth quake in 1988, and since independence was virtually in a state of siege caused by economic blockade by Turkey and Azerbaijan because of the conflict over Nagorono Karabakh region and the prolonged instability of Georgia. This situation cut off the supply routes for imported fuels, on which Armenia was 100 % dependent. This happened when the country's nuclear power plant (2 x 440 MW) remained shut down as a result of the 1988 earth quake. By 1993 the country had an installed power generation capacity of 2744 MW consisting of 988 MW of hydro power stations and 1756 MW of thermal power stations. However, on account of equipment de-rating and water limitations, the available capacity was only about 1971 MW to meet a peak demand of 1788 MW[37]. A 300 MW thermal power plant was under construction, but the progress was slow on account of inadequate funding. Severe lack of fuel resulted in serious shortage of power with most customers getting barely 2 hours of supply everyday. Armenia has no fuel resources of its own. The only primary energy source it has is hydro power; and 40 sites with a total capacity of 700 MW and annual energy of 2200 Gwh have been identified for future development. Transmission is by 220 kV and 110 kV lines and distribution is by 35 kV, 10 kV, 6 kV and 0.4 kV lines. There are about 1.13 million consumers in the country and 350,000 of them are in the capital region of Yerewan.

2.   During 1991-1993, GDP fell by 60% on account of the collapse of FSU, earthquake effects and the conflicts with neighbors. Inflation was at 2,000% in 1992 and 10,000% in 1993. Real wages had declined to $15/month and over 30% of the population came to be classified as poor. The Government undertook a program of economic stabilization, bringing down the fiscal deficit from 48% of GDP in 1993 to 8.4% of GDP in 1996. Inflation was brought down to 6%--the lowest level among all FSU countries-- and GDP started growing again at 5.4% in 1994, 7% in 1995, and 5.8% in 1996. The country has enjoyed a reasonable level of political stability and is trying to improve its relations with Turkey and Azerbaijan. The situation in Georgia has become somewhat normal and physical supply disruptions are no longer a problem. One unit (440 MW) of the nuclear power plant was returned to operation in November 1995. Also the country has cut itself off from the ruble area and issued its own currency achieving a measure of stability its exchange rate regime.

B. The Emergence of the Problem

3.   Power tariffs had to be raised several times to meet the increasing costs of imported fuels as they approached international price levels. Households faced rapidly declining real incomes and even more rapidly rising energy prices. Average households which had only $50/month to spend on all basic needs, had to pay $15 for energy bills. The enterprises faced a sudden loss of domestic markets, and with the collapse of CMEA, the

---

[37] The daily average demand in 1993 was only about 800 MW.

sheltered export markets as well. The severe austerity program under the tight fiscal and monetary policy seriously affected the liquidity of enterprises which started defaulting on their payments to energy companies and the banks. This led to the state owned power company Armenergo defaulting in its payment for gas to the state owned gas company Armgas, which accumulated arrears to the extent of $75 million by 1995 to the gas suppliers in Turkmenistan.

4   Under the "clearing trade" arrangements with Turkmenistan, Armenia paid for the imported gas partly by hard currency and partly by barter (of light industrial products). The import of gas was channeled through a state owned trading company Armturtrade which dealt with 35 Armenian enterprises which provided the goods for the barter. This resulted in the entry of barter payments and practice of set off into the energy sector, leading to a lax payment discipline and non-transparent transactions involving implicit subsidies to the participants. Thus during 1992-95, the situation came to such a pass that only 30% of the bills could be collected in the power sector and only 25% of the collections were in cash. This resulted not only in the inability to import adequate gas and the consequent need to restrict power supply to customers to about 2 hours per day, but also in the lack of cash needed to maintain the power facilities, resulting in a sharp deterioration of the assets.

5.   The government recognized the pervasive nature of the payment problem and its symbiotic linkages to a range of macroeconomic variables and initiated action, even while carrying on the battle to achieve a measure of macroeconomic stability, both under the energy sector and in other areas such as enterprise reform, legal reform, and banking reform to contain the problem. The programs of IMF and the closely coordinated Structural Adjustment Credits I and II of the Bank and the associated Technical assistance credits assisted the government to a great extent in this effort with external funds and analytical support and advice. The two SACs had as their main focus energy sector non-payment problems and energy sector reform.

C. The Change in the Consumption Mix

6.   The Armenian power system was in a dilapidated condition in the early 1990s. It was impossible to cut off power supply to individual low voltage consumers, because of technical reasons relating to radial feeder regimes and the poor condition of switchgear. Illegal supply net works proliferated. There was a lack of consumer and system meters, and the existing ones in apartments in high rise buildings were not accessible to the power utility staff for inspection or for meter reading. The consumption mix had undergone a dramatic change over the two decades resulting in the preponderance of the share of households in the total consumption, as can be seen from the table 1 given below:

Table 1: Change in the Consumption Mix in Power Sector.

Item	1985	1990	1991	1996	1997
Share of Households in the Total Sales (%)	16	23	28	47	50
Share of Industry in the Total Sales (%)	50	32	32	19	17

Source: WB Internal Documents

More than 30% of the consumption by households was by way of power theft, escaping billing and collection efforts. Utility accounting and financial control systems were very poor and consumer accounting was rudimentary. The use of barter and set off became extensive. The accounts receivable in the power sector was reported as being equal to 129 days of sales at the end of 1993. It was clearly on a steep upward swing.

D. Sector Restructuring

7.   The Armenian power system was unbundled in 1995, into generation enterprises, transmission and central load dispatch enterprise and over 70 distribution enterprises later regrouped into 11 distribution enterprises. Armenergo, the former vertically integrated utility, became the enterprise handling transmission and load dispatch functions and it also became the sole buyer of power from the generators following a single purchaser model. It sold power to the Distribution enterprises at different prices, but the end consumer price for the whole country was regulated by the state. Some minor departures were allowed enabling the generators and Armenergo to supply power to a few direct consumers. The quantum of such sales was insignificant. A new Energy Law was enacted in June 1997 giving commercial orientation and operational independence to the energy supply business, allowing private sector entry into the business, defining the policy making role of the government, and providing for independent regulation. An independent regulatory body under the name Energy Commission was set up in June 1997 and started functioning immediately. It was responsible for issuing licenses for carrying on energy supply business and for approving supply tariffs for power, heat and natural gas. The new law also enabled the tariffs (after a two year transition period) to cover all reasonable costs of supply including depreciation on assets revalued in accordance with IAS, interest on borrowed capital, and a competitive return on equity. The unbundled energy enterprises were registered under the newly enacted company law, as joint stock companies. The relationship among the unbundled energy sector entities was to be based on commercial contracts, rather than on the previously adopted system of transfer prices based on central allocation of costs. Since Armenergo was considered more "credit worthy" than the generating companies, it purchased the natural gas from Armgas and gave it to the generators to convert the gas into electricity. Thus Armenergo was in effect paying the generators for the energy conversion only.

E. Approach to Tariffs and Protection of the Poor

8.   In order to cope with the steep increases in fuel costs, the government raised the energy tariffs several times during the years 1994 -1998. The earlier tariffs did not cover fully even the O&M costs; they also allowed cross subsidies compelling industrial consumers to subsidize households, apart from further subsidizing about 20% of the

households belonging to privileged persons, such as government officials, earthquake victims, pensioners etc., to the extent of about 50% of the tariffs. Initially the government changed over to a system of giving subsidies as direct cash payments to a narrowly defined economically vulnerable group of households, getting away from the concept of privileged consumers. Similar cash transfers for other services such as transport and communal services were also introduced. Soon all these cash transfers are expected to be merged into a single vulnerability benefit package aimed at poor households. Tariff increases which came into effect in September 1997 for example raised the average tariff to the end users to about US cents 4.2/kwh compared to the level of US cents 1.4/kwh prevailing in December 1994. At that time, the average tariff for households was only US cents 4.0 / kWh and that for all other consumers including industry was US cents 2.4/ kWh. Under the revised tariffs of September 1997 the average tariff per kWh for the households, industry and "others" rose to US cents 4.4, 4.0 and 5.0 respectively, while adopting a three block tariff for households as shown below:

Table 2: Three Block Tariffs for Households
(including VAT at 20%)

Block	Tariff in US cents/kWh
Life-Line Rate: First 100 kWh/ month	3.0
100 to 250 kWh/ month	4.4
Above 250 kWh/ month	5.0

Source: WB Internal Documents

These tariffs are expected to be further revised upwards in January 1999 (reaching an average tariff/kWh level of US cents 5.1) to recover a part of the debt of the power companies attributable to earlier government policies. Thus while making reasonable efforts to raise tariffs to cover costs of supply, the government has been attempting to protect the weaker sections of the society by life line tariffs and vulnerability benefit package[38]. The approach had been somewhat successful, in combination with other factors, for mitigating the payment problem.

9.   The Government initiated a public awareness campaign to explain that electricity is not an entitlement, but a commodity available only to those who pay for it and also guaranteed that those who pay their power bills would be given at least a supply of 10 to 12 hours everyday compared to the 2 to 3 hours of supply prevailing then. The Ministry of Energy adopted an aggressive policy of control over the system power flows and metering arrangements and did not hesitate to reshuffle the related personnel extensively. Under the Minister's directions control over the financial flows in the system was intensified to prevent leakage. Distribution companies opened numerous collection centers and cash received there was directly transferred to the accounts of the Distribution companies and Armenergo in agreed proportions.

---

[38] About 230,000 households will get income supplements.

F. The Experience of Customer Cooperatives

10.   Initially, to overcome the problem of not being able to cut off power supply to individual households, an experiment supported by TACIS was undertaken to make collections through consumer co-operatives organized for the apartments in high rise buildings and in some cases for all households in a village. The co-operatives elected their own office bearers, who inspected the meters of individual households, collected the dues, retained 8% for their expenses and remitted the rest to the Distribution company collection centers. In many cases advance payments of estimated electricity charges were made to ensure priority in supply. By the end of 1995, all households in Armenia were covered by such arrangements. Each co-operative was electrically isolated and in the event of payment default by any cooperative, power supply to it could be cut off. Collection percentages jumped from the previous levels of about 20 to 30% to the 90% range, largely driven by the anxiety to obtain guaranteed longer hours of supply. It was thus a good experiment in the initial stages. However, the level of improvement in collections could not be sustained for more than a few months. Some of the office bearers of the co-operatives embezzled their collections. In many cases they could not collect dues from 100% of their members, since some members simply did not pay and some openly stole the power bypassing their meters. As a result the Distribution company had to cut off power to the entire co-operative, thus adversely affecting all those who had fully paid their dues. The system therefore came to be abandoned. A view has also been expressed that the margin for the distribution company was adversely affected by this arrangement, thus leading to a lack of enthusiasm on its part to continue the arrangement.

G. Relocation of Meters

11.   Thereafter a decision was taken to move the meters from within the apartment to the first floor or the basement of the apartment building and house them in a locked box, made easily accessible to the staff of the distribution companies. The distribution companies supplied the boxes and locks and the consumers were asked to carry out the task of relocating the meters in the box and associated rewiring at their own cost. The government notified that unless the meter was relocated by a certain date, power supply to the apartment would be cut off. Simultaneously, the laws and rules against theft of power, *inter alia,* by tampering with the locked box of meters, were tightened. This change over to the new system did not meet with any consumer resistance. Most consumers perceived the system as honest and fair and voluntarily complied with the requirements to avoid disconnection and to ensure longer hours of supply.

12.   Distribution companies improved their distribution system to enable disconnection of supply to individual consumes, improved their metering of consumers and low voltage feeders, improved the meter reading practices and also began computerizing consumer records to improve the billing and collection functions. Collections from households improved to the level of 50% in 1996 and 59% in 1997 and are expected to improve more rapidly in 1998.

H. Approach to Budget Entities

13.   Arrears to power companies from the entities financed by the government budget was a significant problem in the early years of the major stabilization effort. To alleviate this, the government established limits of power and heat consumption for each such organization and provided funds in the budget to cover the costs of such authorized consumption. When they exceeded the consumption limit or when they failed to pay their power or heat dues, the power and heat companies were free to disconnect supplies to them. The government also restricted the number of organizations, the power supply to which can not be cut off for default in payment. The government strictly limited the level of consumption by such organizations, when they were in payment default. In such cases the government undertook to settle their bills directly to the power companies within 30 days. All other public entities were subject to disconnection of supply when they fail to pay their bills. Such a policy helped to bring down the arrears from this class of consumers substantially. Collection from budget entities improved to the level of 86% in 1996 and over 96% in 1997.

14.   In 1996 the government's list of entities to which power supply can not be cut consisted of the drinking water supply enterprises and a government owned chemical company (NAIRIT), which was under a program of "care and maintenance" pending its sale to private investors. The drinking water enterprises were required to pay an increasing share of their bills from their own resources, while the government guaranteed the payment of the remaining share of their bills from the budget. Power companies were also allowed to reduce supply of power to the drinking water enterprises in proportion to the amounts not received from them for the previous month. Old arrears from NAIRIT and drinking water companies amounting to $36.5 million to the power companies were adjusted against the power sector debts to the government in respect of gas imports from Turkmenistan, as a part of the Financial Rehabilitation Plan adopted in December 1997 at the suggestion of the Bank.

I. Approach to Industrial Consumers

15.   Arrears from industrial enterprises were sought to be moderated by an aggressive approach to privatization, legal reform and banking reforms. Restrictions on the emerging private sector, and   barriers to foreign investment were dismantled. Laws on real property, registration of real property, banks, banking, collateral, bank insolvency, and commercial bankruptcy as well as a comprehensive and modern company law were enacted. Civil code was improved to enable companies to own the property they were occupying. Most prices were liberalized and state trading was abolished. Foreign investment, foreign trading and foreign exchange regimes were liberalized. Legal and regulatory framework for capital markets were put in place and three stock exchanges came into operation. Laws on securities and capital market regulating authorities are being enacted.

16.   The program of privatizing all small scale enterprises (about 7700 in all) has been completed by December 1997. By that time 1864 large and medium enterprises have been offered for sale. The privatization of the remaining enterprises is expected to be completed by the year 2000. Making use of the combination of privatization, liquidation

and bankruptcy procedures, the government is making an attempt to make the industrial sector viable. Related banking reforms included the restructuring the insolvent ones, subjecting them to prudential regulations relating capital adequacy, loan loss provisioning and tight supervision by the central bank. As a result the ratio of non-performing assets to total assets has come down from 25% to 15%. The power company and the banks jointly arrange for the restructuring of the insolvent companies and rescheduling their debts. Adoption of the IAS based accounting and audit is being introduced in all sectors.

17.   The measures taken by the government to increase cash collections include: (a) ban on the use of the tax set off, except in respect of the one-on-one type in which the value of the transaction is transparent and verifiable; and (b) limiting barter transactions to a minimum of 25% for electricity payments and 30% for gas payments. The most recent measures taken by the government include: (a) the separation of the functions of meter reading and bill preparation; and (b) bill payment through banks rather than through utility staff. In areas where these two measures were implemented, a steep increase in the collection ratio was noticed.

J. Collection Results

18.   As a result of these concerted efforts covering all classes of consumers, the collection performance and the share of cash collections have registered notable improvements. Power supply has been restored to 24 hours/ day basis to all consumers compared to the 2 to 4 hours/day supply prevailing in 1993 and 1994. Collection results of 1996 are summarized below:

Table 3: Collection Performance in 1996 at Different Levels of the Power Sector

Item	At the Distribution Company Level	At the Transmission Company Level	At the Generation Company Level
Total Collection as a % of Billing	65.1	50.9	26.3
Cash as a % of Total Collections	59.8	66.8	9.7
Barter/ Set off as a % of Total Collections	40.2	33.2	90.3

Source: WB Internal Documents

Consumer category wise payment performance 1996 is summarized in the following table.

Table 4: Payment Performance of Consumer Categories in 1996

Consumer Category	Sales in GWh	Share in Sales (%)	Payment as a % of Bills.
Households	2095	47.1	50
Industry[39]	859	19.3	98
Budget Entities	292	6.6	86
Water Supply and Transport	465	10.5	74
Agriculture	303	6.8	15
Others	430	9.7	68
Total	4444	100.0	65

Source: WB Internal Documents

19. The performance in 1997 had been somewhat similar. The overall collection efficiency at the level of Distribution companies is 62%. Cash collections amounted to 64% of the total collections. The payment performance of different categories of consumers in 1997 is summarized in the following table.

Table 5: Payment Performance of Consumer Categories in 1997

Consumer Category	Sales in GWh	Share in Sales (%)	Payment as a % of Bills.
Households	2175	49.5	57.8
Industry	731	16.6	71.3
Budget entities	340	7.7	96.1
Drinking Water Companies.	301	6.8	52.5
Agriculture & Irrigation	277	6.4	11.5
Transport	153	3.5	95.1
Others	416	9.5	60.3
Total	4393	100.0	62.0

Source: WB Internal Documents

At the end of 1997, the transmission company Armenergo is reported to have paid 80 % of the non fuel dues to the Generation companies, apart from having paid for the import of natural gas. While there is no doubt that there has been a significant increase in collections from the levels experienced in 1993-95, the collection performance seem to have leveled off somewhat at around 60 % . It is not possible for any power company to survive at this level of collection. Collection percentages should be in the high nineties and lot more of work is to be done to achieve that level.

K. Tasks for the Immediate Future

20. While the technical transmission and distribution losses are at about 18.5% of net generation, theft losses are believed to be in the range of 15 to 20%. Comprehensive efforts are still required to stop theft. A wide range of households still do not pay their bills and a combination of technical reasons and corrupt practices of the utility staff effectively wards off disconnection for non-payment. A good portion of the collected funds are misappropriated and do not reach the accounts of the distribution or transmission companies. Anecdotal evidence suggests that this is an informal but perhaps a well organized effort. The defaults from drinking water companies, agriculture

---

[39] Includes direct sales of 47.31 Gwh by generating companies to direct consumers.

and irrigation tend to be chronic and call for a major and bold policy break through in cost recovery based pricing in those sectors. Reform work in the near future will have to focus on these sectors. Removal of the remaining inefficiencies in the power sector might be possible only by resorting to privatization of the distribution entities through sale of controlling shares to strategic investors in order to improve substantially the quality of corporate governance and management controls. The government plans to carry out such a privatization through a tendering process during 1999-2000. Adherence to IAS based accounting and independent external audit is also a matter of high priority.

L. Impact on the Gas Sector

21.   The improved collections in the power sector has improved the collection in the gas sector, as power generation consumes 75% of the imported natural gas. Armgas is thus able to buy increasing quantities of gas, by being able to pay for it. Certain reforms carried out by the government in respect of gas imports are also noteworthy. The role of the state trading company Armturtrade has been eliminated and Armgas has emerged as the sole importer. No state owned enterprise would be allowed to accumulate arrears to Armgas. Armgas will enter into the gas purchase transaction without any government guarantee and payments for the purchase of gas have to be made by Armgas from a separate account to which funds can only come from: (a) payments from gas customers; (b) sale of assets by Armgas; and (c) credits guaranteed by the government subject to a maximum of $6 million at any time. Armgas will buy gas only to the extent it can pay for it in cash. If it decides to buy for barter, then the goods must be paid for in cash from the special account mentioned above. These arrangements have brought greater discipline and transparency to gas purchase transactions. Armgas has thus achieved a reasonable level of liquidity enabling it to remain current in its payments to Turkmenistan, except for occasional rescheduling of payments to tide over the monthly fluctuations of its revenue stream.

22.   Energy sector debts to the government to the extent of $12.5 million have been partly set off against debts to the sector by NAIRIT chemicals and the drinking water supply companies and by the government assuming as sovereign debt the payments to Russia of $3.4 million for nuclear fuel, as a part of the Bank recommended Financial Rehabilitation Plan. The remaining debt of about $25 million would be during 1998-1999 through suitable rescheduling. To increase the ability of the power sector to pay such arrears, tariffs were revised upwards in April 1998.

M. Lessons from the Case

23.   Bank staff estimate that the deficits in the energy sector arising from losses and theft, inadequate tariffs and inefficient collection to be of the order of 4 to 5% of GDP, which is comparable to the fiscal deficit target of 4.5 to 5.5% of GDP agreed with IMF. In this context, the experience in Armenia highlights the efficacy of a comprehensive approach involving macroeconomic stabilization, improvement of legal infrastructure, reform of the banking sector, stepping up the pace of privatization , accelerating the liquidation of insolvent and bankrupt companies in conjunction with sectoral reforms (tariff reform, removal of subsidies and cross subsidies, targeted social assistance, unbundling of the sector, independent regulation, and upgrading of the utility practices)

in mitigating the payment problem at least partially in the context of a difficult and turbulent transition to market economy. Reasonable political stability, unitary state, and the existence of a homogenous and cohesive ethnic population had been favorable factors. Perhaps its import dependence for fuel is a blessing in disguise, but it is still open to debate. What is clear however is that multilateral assistance by way of well coordinated IMF programs and the Bank's adjustment and investment lending and non financial services focusing on the sector reform in conjunction with macro economic stabilization, helps to develop a better understanding of the problem and deal with it effectively.

REFERENCES

1. Armenia: Energy Sector Review, June 1993
2. SAR : Armenia Power Maintenance Project, November 1994
3. President's Report: Armenia Structural Adjustment Credit I, January 1996
4. President's Report: Armenia Structural Adjustment Credit II August 1997
5. Armenia: Country Assistance Strategy, July 1997
6. Supervision Report dated 17 December 1997
7. President's Memorandum to Board dated 29 December 1997 regarding the release of the final tranche of the SAC II
8. Draft Appraisal documents dated 18 March 1998 for the proposed Power Transmission and Distribution Project in Armenia
9. Notes of Ms. Nina Bubnova on the status of collections in Armenia, July 1998

THE LITHUANIAN CASE STUDY

A. Background

1.   Lithuania is one of the few ECA countries, which appear to have largely succeeded in containing an emerging non-payment problem in energy sector from growing into a large one affecting macro-economic management. This case study attempts to identify the policies pursued and steps taken, as well as the conditions under which they were successful.

2.   Lithuania is a compact nation of modest size and a population of 3.8 million. It is also a unitary state with a cohesive population (over 80% is of Lithuanian origin) and not a federation of many states and ethnic groups pulling in different directions. Its natural resource endowments are modest and it has to import almost all of its fuel requirements. Its industrial and energy infrastructure established when it was part of FSU, became characterized by excess capacity upon its becoming independent. In the context of regional economic transition, its imported input prices (especially those of fuels) quickly rose to internationally traded levels, while its traditional export markets such as FSU considerably shrank in size.

3.   As in the case of other FSU states, the transition in Lithuania was painful. The GDP fell by 50% during 1990-1993. Annual inflation was running at 1020% in 1992. Major employment problems arising from the severe contraction in industrial output had to be handled. The successive democratic governments were responsive to suggestions on difficult macroeconomic choices to be made under the two IMF standby agreements in 1992 and 1993, a EEF loan from IMF in 1994, a SAL of the Bank in 1996 and significant balance of payment support and substantial technical assistance grants from G-24 countries. Following a stabilization program involving strict fiscal discipline, tight credit and income policies inflation was brought under control by mid 1994 and to the level of single digits by 1997. The annualized inflation rate. estimated in April 98, is of the order of 6.9%. GDP growth resumed in 1994 and the real growth registered during 1995-1997 was in the range of 3 to 5%. Exchange rate stability was ensured, inter alia, by the interim measure of establishing a Currency Board which pegged and maintained the exchange rate at $ 1.0 = Lt. 4.0. Fiscal deficit has been contained at 1% of GDP and the government hopes to balance its budget in 1999. Interest rates have come down and presently 90- day treasury bill rates are less than 10%. Pursuit of such sound macroeconomic policies was complemented by the adoption of largely sensible sectoral policies, though characterized often by hesitation and occasional reversal inevitable in a democratic regime.

B. Energy Sector Dimensions and Institutions

4.   The country's power system had an installed generation capacity of 5178 MW including the Ignalina Nuclear Power Plant (NPPI) with a capacity of 3000 MW, derated on account of safety reasons to 2500 MW, a thermal power station with 1800 MW, three CHP plants with a total of 772 MW and a run-of-the-river hydro plant of 106 MW. In

addition to these there is 4 x 200 MW pumped storage hydro plant at Kruonis. The demand for electricity which plunged along with the contraction of GDP during 1990-93 is recovering at the rate of about 4% per year since 1994. Still the peak demand is only around 2000 MW, leading to an excessive reserve capacity margin. The CHP plants of the power system supply about 30% of the heat for the district heating systems, which get the remaining 70% of the heat from the several heat only boilers (HOB) located near the load centers. The total annual production of heat is around 100 PJ [40], 25% of which is in the form of steam for industrial consumers and the rest in the form of hot water for space heating and for direct use. The heat consumption dropped by about 50% during 1990-95, though consumption by households registered an increase of about 8% during the same period. Natural gas pipe lines with a transmission capacity of 14 billion cubic meters per year(bcm/y) transport gas from Russia to Lithuania (through Belaruss) and they are also used to transmit gas to Kaliningrad and Latvia for which Lithuania charges transit fees. The gas consumption fell from about 6 bcm/y in 1990 to about 2.5 bcm/y in 1995. Oil is received from Russia through pipelines and the refinery at Mazeikiai has a throughput capacity of 13 million tonnes/year (mt/y). During 1990-95 the oil consumption in the country fell by 67% and the oil sector facilities were correspondingly underutilized.

5.   The Ministry of Energy is administratively responsible for the sector and supervises the various energy sector entities which are mostly state owned enterprises with a special status which enables a greater level of intervention (when necessary) than in other ordinary SOEs. The Ignalina Nuclear Power Plant is a separate entity which sells all its generated power to   Lithuanian Power Company (LPC) which owns the remaining generating units and the transmission and distribution systems. The generating units and the seven distribution systems are organized as fully owned subsidiaries[41] of LPC. The CHP plants and HOBs and the associated heat distribution systems, till recently owned by LPC[42], are now owned by the municipalities either directly or through fully owned subsidiaries. Lithuanian Gas (LG) owns the gas transmission facilities and distributes gas through 10 gas distributing companies. Lithuanian Fuel (LF) distributes the refined oil products through 13 distribution companies. The refinery at Mazeikiai and the oil terminal at Klaipeda (which exports excess oil products) are organized as separate companies.

C. Emergence of the Non-Payment Problem

6.   Lithuania had been following an administered price system for energy. Since 1982, the government (the office of Pricing and Competition in the Ministry of Economy) was setting prices on the basis of evaluated costs of production in the government owned energy entities covering the costs of fuel, transmission and distribution as well as depreciation and a 10% return on the substantially understated and historically valued rate base. The resulting tariffs were very low by international comparison. Industrial

---

[40] Peta Joules that is 10 to the power of 15 joules.

[41] However, they do not pay tax , and do not file financial statements, separately. LPC produces a consolidated balance sheet and pays tax.

[42] Till very recently, LPC was responsible for district heating throughout the country and it was operating through several regional systems.

consumers subsidized the residential consumers substantially in the power and gas sectors, and in the district heating such cross subsidization was even more pronounced. The basic principle was to keep the energy entities solvent through periodic adjustment of the prices and to compensate the entities for losses sustained to the extent such losses were caused by inadequate or delayed tariff revisions. During the economic turmoil of the early 1990s, when the imported fuel prices rose dramatically to international levels, energy demand fell and excess capacities came into existence, the government's response was to allow market prices for traded energy goods (oil and oil products, coal and LPG), and continue to adopt the administered price formula for non-traded energy such as electricity, gas and district heating. Since this led to steep increases in tariffs, the government dragged their feet somewhat and the price revisions became less and less punctual, calling for compensatory payments to LPC (or production subsidies as they were called). Still the resulting heat tariffs for industrial consumers proved so high that many of them disconnected from the district heating system and resorted to alternative methods of producing heat and steam. This made the district heating systems even more uneconomic, calling for higher tariffs or greater production subsidies. Supply of heat from the district heating system to households was unmetered and was charged on the basis of the size of the house and the number of people living there. It was estimated that households paid 26% of the single salary income for all utility services--3% for power, 15% for heating, and 8% for other utilities. Even then these tariffs produced revenues to cover no more than 30% of the supply costs.

7.   It is under these circumstances the problem of non-payment emerged. LPC started accumulating arrears from power and heat consumers. By end 1993 LPC's receivable from power consumers was equivalent to 47 days sales, while its receivable from heat consumers rose to the level of 110 days sales. By 1996 the energy sector arrears reached the level of Lt. 380 million (Lt. 350 million for power and heat and Lt. 50 million for gas) equivalent to 51 days sales. More than 50% of these dues were from the government budget entities and municipalities and the rest was owed by household and agricultural consumers. Government's own arrears in respect of subsidies payable to LPC for power and heat amounted to Lt. 772 million for the 1994-96 period. LPC's arrears to LG for gas supplies amounted to Lt. 60 million and LG owed Lt.110 million to Russian gas suppliers, who threatened to disrupt gas supplies, if payment was further delayed.

D. Government's Response

(1) Tariff Adjustments

8.   The government reacted to these developments in many ways at different points in time. In retrospect the government's approach could be summarized as follows. To meet increasing input costs, first the tariff of industrial power consumers was raised and latter the power tariff for households was also raised to a level matching the industrial tariffs. Since a similar approach to heat tariffs resulted in heat tariffs for households which was perceived to be beyond their affordability, heat tariffs were sought to be subsidized by power tariffs by calculating the latter based on higher than normal returns and calculating the former on the basis of lower than normal returns. The district heating system does not enable easy disconnection of individual households and also does not provide meters for them. The households have, therefore, no way of reducing their consumption in response to price signals. Thus the government ended up by subsidizing the household heat consumers in at least three ways. Subsidy by the industrial heat consumers, production subsidy to the heat supplier for not giving it an economic tariff (or alternately allowing higher power prices to subsidize the heat prices) and subsidy by the state to the poorer sections of the consumers. Since a significant number of industrial heat consumers reacted to higher prices by switching over to alternative methods of heating, the first option became unpractical. In the context of the heat supply business being decentralized to municipalities, cross subsidy of heat tariffs by power tariffs would no longer be a viable option. Finally the government came around to the concept of setting heat tariffs based on supply costs and subsidizing from the state budget those heat consumers who had to spend more than 15% of their income on space heating (and 5% on hot water supplies) circumscribed by the size of the house and the number of people living there. Thus by 1996 the power and heat tariffs for households were actually higher than those of industries.

Table 1: Reform of Household tariffs for Heat and Power
(Average for the year in US cents)

Consumer Category	Units	Tariff in 1995	Tariff in 1996
A. Power tariffs:			
Industry	kWh	3.29	3.45
Households	kWh	3.95	4.21
Other	kWh	4.00	4.38
B. Heat Tariffs			
Industry	Giga Calorie	18.88	20.78
Households	Giga Calorie	12.94	22.44
Others	Giga Calorie	18.56	20.22

Source: WB Internal Documents

Such an approach actually cost the state less, since the consumer subsidy scheme progressively redistributes the higher heat bills towards those who do not qualify for the subsidy (higher income households and others). Consumer subsidy payments in 1997 was estimated at $50 million.

(2) Cost Cutting Thrust

9.   Since the tariff was based on the "cost plus" approach, a cost cutting thrust in the sector policy assumed significance. The main elements of this thrust were: (a) the organization of the energy entities as fully corporatized joint stock companies to enable better corporate governance and to reduce government involvement in operational matters; (b) requiring them to adopt International Accounting Standards, transparent accounts and external audit; (c) management performance improvement through management performance audits; (d) appointment of supervisory boards to improve the oversight function; (e) decentralization of the district heating assets and functions from LPC to the municipalities; and (f) accelerating the privatization of the oil sector entities and the non-core activities from other energy entities.

(3) Disconnection Policy

10.   In order to nip in the bud the emerging problem of non-payments, the government passed a law enabling the energy entities to impose sanctions on consumers who accumulate arrears to the suppliers of electricity, gas or heat. These included disconnection of the service, imposition of penalties and recourse to courts for recovery of arrears. Unlike in the case of power supply, the district heating systems did not provide meters for household consumers. Nor was it possible to disconnect the consumer from the heating system due to its technical limitations. The government therefore ordered that LPC could disconnect power supply to those consumers who default in their payments for heat supply. This novel method was conceivable in the context of both power supply and heat supply being handled by LPC. After the decentralization of heating systems to the municipalities, this did not prove to be a viable option. In any case, disconnection of heat and power supply to households in winter months was not a very practical proposition. Nonetheless these laws strengthened the hands of the energy supply entities in their collection drives.

(4) Direct Adjustment of Municipal Arrears

11.   The 1997 budget legislation included a section to the effect that when the power and heat arrears of any municipality (or any entity funded from the budget of a municipality) exceeded the equivalent of 30 days worth of billing, the government was authorized to pay the excess arrears directly to LPC from the amounts provided in the state budget for transfers to the relevant municipality. The Ministry of Finance operationalized the law through a decree enabling a mechanism of monthly monitoring of such arrears and payment of excess arrears directly to LPC.

(5) Enforcement of Payment Discipline on Government Entities

12.   The said legislation also enabled the government to take firm action against government budget entities which defaulted in their payments to LPC for heat and power. The government followed a system of agreeing with each department head the volume of heat and power to be consumed by the entities under his supervision and made earmarked provision in the department's budget to pay for such energy consumption. The heads of departments were obliged to ensure that the actual consumption was within the budgeted

limits and that the earmarked provision was used only for the payment of energy bills, and not diverted for any other use. Based on the provisions of the budget law, the government also authorized LPC to disconnect service and apply other appropriate sanctions in respect of budget entities which still defaulted in payments and accumulated arrears exceeding 30 days worth of billing. This was not applicable only to hospitals, laboratories and similar institutions which would suffer damage to microbiological samples etc., if power supply is disconnected. However even the heads of these institutions were put on notice that non-payment of energy bills by diverting the budget provision for other uses would result in disciplinary proceedings against them and eventually to their dismissal from service. The government also decided to publish the names of heads of organizations who default in their energy payments and to initiate action for their dismissal. Finally actual disconnection of some high profile customers such as the street lighting system in the capital of the country had the desired demonstration effect.

13.   As a result of these measures the receivable from the state budget entities came down from the equivalent of 82 days billings in April 97 to about 32 days of billing in September 1997. Municipal debts dropped from 86 days billing to 21 days of billing during the same period. The extent of reduction in arrears during the one year period August 1996- September 1997 can be gauged from the following table.

Table 2: Levels of Energy Sector Accounts Receivable in Equivalent Days of Sales

Customer Category	A/R as of August 1, 1996	A/R as of September 1, 1997
A. Electricity		
All Consumers	42	13
Government Budget Entities	153	32
Municipal Budget Entities	284	21
B. Heat		
All Consumers	51	34
Government Budget Entities	97	29
Municipal Budget Entities	196	56
C. Natural Gas		
Government Budget Entities	95	53
LPC	134	3

Source: WB Internal Documents

14.   In the last quarter of 1997, the government transferred all the district heating assets, operation and responsibilities from LPC to the municipalities. To prevent the municipalities from financing their deficits through arrears to their own district heating subsidiaries, the government continued to monitor the arrears situation and direct settlement from government budget. A suitable section has been inserted in the 1998 budget law-- this time favoring only the district heating entities. By maintaining pressure in this manner, the accounts receivable level has been further brought down in 1997. At the end of 1997 the accounts receivable level was 13 days for power sector, 33 days for district heating and 46 days for natural gas.

(6) Establishment of A Regulatory Body

15.   In November 1996, the government also established by law the Energy Price Commission (EPC) as an autonomous body to regulate the prices of electricity, gas and district heating. Five commissioners were appointed and EPC commenced its work in February 1997 and approved revised tariffs for power, heat and gas based on the recovery of full cost principle. These tariffs came into effect by July 97. The tariff setting procedure was thus largely depoliticised. The management performance audit of the energy entities is expected to provide the EPC with bench marks and efficiency norms for further refining of the tariff setting process.

(7) Settlement of Inter- Enterprise Arrears

16.   The government budget for 1997 also provided a sum of Lt.100 million for clearing the arrears to LPC built up by the government budget entities in 1996. This amount was disbursed to LPC in 4 installments in 1997. Similarly compensatory payments to LPC (for not having set tariffs to cover costs of supply during the period January 1994- October 1996) amounting to Lt.776 million was also approved by the parliament in December 1996 and was settled (through a government decree issued in April 1997) by adjusting taxes owed by LPC to the government, by the government taking over the obligations of LPC in respect of certain debts of LPC and by cash payments to LPC amounting to Lt. 137 million. The parliament has recognized a similar compensatory payment for the first half of 1997 amounting to Lt. 131 million for LPC and it will be paid out soon. With the adoption of EPC recommended tariffs based on full cost recovery, the practice of paying production subsidies from the government budget will be given up. In order to protect the poorer sections of the populations from the tariffs set on this basis, the government budget for 1998 includes provisions amounting to Lt. 203 million which will be disbursed as consumer subsidies (see paragraph 8).

17.   Thus by the end of 1997 LPC cleared all its debts to NPPI, LF and LG. LG was able to clear its arrears to Gazprom of Russia for gas imports. LPC was also able to collect its arrears from its importers of power by adopting a tough disconnection stance and diplomacy.

E. Lessons from Lithuanian Experience

18.   The key elements of the Lithuanian strategy clearly are: (i) scrupulous adherence to the principle of keeping the energy entities solvent by (a) giving them a tariff designed to recover full cost of service; (b) paying production subsidies to energy entities for losses sustained by them on account of delayed or inadequate tariffs approved by the government; and (c) providing consumer subsidies where the tariffs set on the full cost recovery principle results in tariffs not affordable by the poorer sections of the society; (ii) giving autonomy (free from political interference) to energy entities to disconnect supplies to the defaulting customers and recover the dues; (iii) enforcing payment discipline on the part of government entities through earmarked and adequate provisions in the government budget for energy payments and subjecting them to the disconnection and sanctions by LPC; and (iv) direct settlement by the government of the dues of defaulting municipalities from the funds in the state budget destined for transfers to

municipalities. None of these are novel or new solutions unknown in other countries. The noteworthy factor is the political will and consensus built up in a democratic framework for stern adherence to these elements. Also noteworthy is the manner in which the policy dichotomy between macroeconomic management and sectoral management (one comes across in most countries) has been avoided. The temptation to use government arrears to the energy system as financing to cover fiscal deficits in the context of adopting harsh fiscal and monetary policies to control runaway inflation appears to have been resisted by developing an understanding of the need for elimination of fiscal deficits in the context of eliminating deficits in the broader quasi- public sector such as banking, energy, agriculture and social security with close linkages to fiscal balance.

19.   Though commendable, the gains are still fragile. The problem is contained but not eliminated. It can rear its head again the moment there is slack of budget discipline. Recent proposals to add to the membership of EPC part-time and voting representatives of trade unions and industry, and the continuing need for the proposals of EPC to be approved by the Cabinet are areas for correction. To consolidate the gains so far achieved, the government needs to pursue seriously the meaningful privatization of the energy entities, ensuring that shareholding patterns enable a corporate profit maximization motive and management improvements and behavior induced by such a motive.

REFERENCES

1.   Lithuania Energy Sector Review, May 1994
2.   SAR of Lithuania Power Rehabilitation Project May 1994
3.   Lithuania Country Assistance Strategy, November 1994
4.   President's Report & Recommendation, SAL to Lithuania, September 1996
5.   Lithuania: An Opportunity for Economic Success , Draft Report dated April 1998
6.   Back-to-office-reports of supervision missions for SAL dated October 1997 and May 1998
7.   1997 Lithuanian Budget Law

THE CASE STUDY OF GEORGIA

A. Economic Background

1.   Georgia is one of the FSU states which has realized the seriousness of the non-payment problem and is making some determined efforts to overcome it with some signs of initial improvement. This case study takes note of the difficulties faced by Georgia, the steps taken by it and the results so far achieved, and also points out the key items of work yet to be addressed or followed through.

2.   With a population of 5.4 million and an area of 70,000 square kms, Georgia was one of the wealthy republics of the Soviet Union. Upon becoming independent in April 1991, it was entangled in a civil war caused by the secessionist movement of the Abkhazia and South Ossetia provinces (A and SO) and also in internal armed conflicts. Cease-fire came towards the end of 1993, but the war and political turmoil took a heavy toll on the economy, which was also facing the consequences of the political and economic breakdown of the FSU as well as the dismantling of CEMA arrangements.

3.   During 1990-1994, the GDP of the country in real terms dropped by more than 70%; real wages declined by about 90%; and external debt rose to $1.0 billion or 200% of the country's merchandise exports in 1994. Inflation which ran at an annual rate of 131% in 1991, rose to 7488% in 1993 and remained at 6473% in 1994. Fiscal deficit as a percentage of GDP rose to 26.2 %. Broad money was at the level of 31.3% of GDP in 1992. By 1994 unemployment rose to a high level of 20%.

4.   Serious reform efforts commenced in mid 1994 under the IMF and World Bank programs. The stabilization effort involved the use of tight fiscal and monetary policies to rein in inflation. Other key components of the reform included the overall attempts to improve the environment for the functioning of private sector, attempts to eliminate subsidies, liberalization of most prices and trade, downsizing of the budget financed entities, completion of the privatization of the small enterprises, enactment of the basic legal framework, land reforms, as well as some aspects of banking and energy sector reforms. Lari was introduced as the country's national currency in April 1995 paving the way for some currency stability.

5.   As a result , by the end of 1996, fiscal deficit came down to about 5% of GDP, and the annual rate of inflation slowed down to 14%. The current account deficit came down from 34% of GDP in 1994 to 8% in 1996, based on a 20% export growth. GDP decline bottomed out in 1994 and real growth rates of 2.5% in 1995 and 10.5% in 1996 were registered. Growth rate in 1997 was also at the high level of 10.5 to 11%.

B. Energy Sector Dimensions

6.   Georgia's domestic energy resource endowments are modest. Its hydroelectric potential is estimated at 87 Twh and about 10% of this has been developed. Its modest oil and coal reserves have been nearly exhausted and local production has shrunk considerably. By 1994 the country's indigenous supplies (mostly hydro and wood fuels) could cover only 32% of its energy needs. Foreign exchange shortage hampered the

imports of fuel and power causing acute energy shortages in the country. Civil war and internal strife had damaged power generation and transmission facilities reducing domestic generation and making it physically difficult to handle power imports to load centers.

7.   Georgia, along with Armenia and Azerbaijan was a part of the Trans Caucasian Interconnected Power System-- one of 11 such systems in FSU--, which upon dissolution of FSU, split into three unbalanced national systems. In Georgia most of the generating capacity was in the west, while the load centers were in the east and the only east west transmission link tended to become overloaded causing instability. Abkhazia and South Ossetia provinces consumed in 1995, some 825 Gwh of electricity at the distribution level or 13% of the country's total electricity consumption. Most of it was imported from Russia and the Government of Georgia had to assume the payment obligations to Russia, while the country's power utility, Sakenergo was not allowed to collect the power dues from these provinces. The 1300 MW storage hydro power station at Inguri in the Abkhazia province is damaged and is in need of urgent rehabilitation.

8.   The nominal installed generation capacity in Georgia is 5090 MW, comprising 2088 MW of large thermal power stations, 2843 MW of hydropower stations, 5.4 MW of diesel generating sets, and 153 MW of industrial captive plants. The thermal plants are at Gardabani (10 units, 1850 MW), Tkvarcheli (2 units. 220 MW) and Tiblisi (3 units of CHP, 18 MW). The hydro capacity consists of 103 power stations with 182 units, of which 6 are large storage hydro stations, 17 are large run-of-river stations, and the rest are small run-of-river stations. On account of war damages and inability to rehabilitate and maintain them for want of funds, the available capacity is limited to 400 MW of thermal power and 400 to 1000 MW hydro power depending on water availability. Compared to a theoretical energy capability of 10,000 Gwh, the hydro plants could produce only 4500 Gwh in 1994. One estimate puts the available capacity at 2600 MW in 1996 compared to a peak demand of 1500 MW and base demand of 600 MW.

9.   Georgian transmission system has 500 kV (572 kms), 330 kV (21 kms), 220 kV (1565 kms) and 110 kV (4210 kms) lines and interconnections to Armenia, Azerbaijan and Russia with a total transfer capacity of 3000 MVA. Russia exports power to Turkey via Georgia and pays to the latter wheeling charges for the same. The National Dispatch Center at Tiblisi is backed by a regional one at Kutaisi and 17 other local dispatch centers. The country was divided into 66 distribution areas[43] receiving power from 21 major substations. Sub transmission is by 35 kV lines while primary distribution is by 10 kV and 6 kV lines (20,500 kms). The secondary distribution is by 0.4 kV lines (53,000 kms). Excluding those in A and SO provinces there are over 1.2 million customers and 98 % of them are households. The system had one million single phase meters and 50,000 three phase meters covering about 90% of the consumers. The meters are over 30 years old; one third of them are defective and one eighth of them are believed to have been tampered with. Most of them are located inside the apartments and a third of them are

---

[43] There are 12 districts and 64 administrative regions in the country.

94

believed not to have been sealed[44]. Replacement of meters is hampered for want of cash flow in the system.

C. Decline in Demand and Supply Constraints

10.   Because of the political and economic turmoil, the demand for electricity declined from 14.2 TWh in 1989 to 4.3 TWh in 1997 (see Table 1)and yet the system was unable to meet the demand, because of the poor condition of the generation, transmission and distribution facilities, which could not be rehabilitated and maintained properly in the absence of adequate collections.

Table 1: Georgia Electricity Demand and Supply
(Data in TWh unless otherwise stated)

Item	1989	1990	1994	1997
Net Generation	14.703	14.198	6.494	6.400
Net Imports	2.260	3.204	0.868	0.150
Total Supply	16.963(100%)	17.402(100%)	7.362(100%)	6.550(100%)
Transmission Losses	1.951(11.5%)	2.001(11.5%)	2.207 (29.9%)	1.800 (27.5%)
Distribution Losses	0.826 (4.8%)	0.924 (5.3%)	0.498 (6.8%)	0.475(7.3%)
Net Consumption	14.187(100%)	14.447(100%)	4.656 (100%)	4.275 (100%)
Share of Industry (%)	6.530 (46%)	5.910 (41%)	0.926 (20%)	0.983 (23%)
Share of Households (%)	2.420 (17%)	2.320 (16%)	2.818 (61%)	2.445 (57%)
Share of Others (%)	5.327 (37%)	6.247 (43%)	0.912 (20%)	0.846 (20%)

Source: WB Internal Documents

Note: 1. Transmission and distribution losses are expressed as percentages of total supply in parentheses. 2. Shares of industry, households and others are expressed as percentages of Net consumption in parentheses. 3. Transmission losses in 1990-97 include about 750 Gwh of supplies to Abkhazia and South Ossetia provinces.

The lack of revenues also hampered purchase of fuel and often had led to wage arrears as well. Even in Tbilisi, the nation's capital, even now power outages of 2 to 18 hours duration are frequent. Apart from the overall decline in demand, the share of industrial consumption in total consumption has declined from 46% in 1989 to 235 in 1997, while the share of households rose from 17% to 55% during the same period. Supply disruptions in the gas sector and the collapse of district heating systems also led the households using electricity for cooking and space heating with inefficient appliances, especially in winter 1994. The transmission and distribution losses were at 16.3% in 1989 have risen to 34.8% in 1997, partly because of the inclusion of about 750 Gwh of supplies to the A and SO provinces as transmission loss. Even allowing for this the losses have risen to about 23.3%, which is high. This is due to inappropriate loading of the system, poor maintenance of lines and substations and a rise in theft of power, as well as defective metering and billing.

---

[44] The data is basically from the Telasi distribution company which handles 50% of the country's power sales and 33% of the country's total number of customers.

D. Emergence of the Payment Problem and Government's Response

11.   As in other FSU states, the economic and political turmoil during 1989-94 resulted in considerable non-payment of dues in the electricity sector of Georgia. Lack of markets and tight fiscal and monetary policies led to the default by insolvent industrial units, government budget entities (GBEs) and quasi budget entities such as the agencies handling water supply, sewerage and transport. The problem in respect of the households was the most acute in Georgia. Apart from the problem of not being able to collect anything at all from the A and SO provinces, the large number of refugees who moved from these areas to the rest of Georgia could not pay for any of the services including electricity. People were particularly hard hit by steep declines in personal incomes (90%), high levels of unemployment (20%) and inflation (four digits) and rising electricity prices perceived to be wholly inconsistent with the acute shortages and poor quality and duration (as low as two hours per day) of power supply. Disruption in gas supply and district heating forced the people to use electricity beyond the levels of their affordability. This resulted in a steep drop in the collections from households. Overall collections were at 20-25% during 1993-95, and reached a low of 20% of billings in 1995. Lack of legal framework to prosecute those who stole power and to disconnect supplies to the defaulting consumers was a major problem in the earlier years. In any case political interference at the local levels nipped in the bud any attempt to disconnect supplies to the defaulting customers.

12.   Government's response was conceived within the reform framework commenced since mid-1994. It took initiatives to improve the organization and accountability in the sector, attempted to enforce the practice of supply disconnection as a remedy for non-payment, and took steps to create growing consumer awareness of the commercial nature of the power supply arrangements. With the help of multilateral and bilateral donors, the government has initiated the rehabilitation of some power facilities. A Ministry of Fuels and Energy was reestablished in June 1996, and a Presidential decree was issued in July 1996 declaring the intention of the government to unbundle and restructure the power sector to enable the eventual privatization of the corporatized power sector entities, to introduce accounting and management reforms in the sector and to undertake the implementation of a financial recovery plan for the sector entities. Under the financial recovery plan, the government partly settled the accumulated stock of debts in the sector. As of 30 June 1996, both the accounts receivable and accounts payable of Sakenergo stood at the level of about Lari 285 million. They were reduced by about 50% through: (a) the government assuming the debt of Lari 96 million payable to Iran and Turkmenistan for fuel imports; and (b) transferring to a newly established Government body called Energia Plus both the arrears of Lari 36 million from the consumers of A and SO provinces and the debt payable to Russia for the import of electricity for these provinces. The remaining accounts payable and receivable of Sakenergo were restructured to be liquidated in three years.

13.   In June 1997 a new electricity law was enacted to provide the legal and commercial framework for the unbundling and restructuring of the sector going on since late 1995 and to provide the legal basis for the punitive action against power theft and non-payments. Further the law enabled the creation of an independent regulatory body for the power sector with authority to grant licenses and regulate tariffs. Meanwhile tariffs were

adjusted upwards several times and attempts made to rationalize and reduce subsidies. Sector unbundling commenced from late 1995, when Sakenergo, which was till then a vertically integrated utility, was split into two generation enterprises, a transmission and load dispatch enterprise and 66 distribution enterprises. "Sakenergo generation" owned and operated most hydro power stations and all thermal power stations except the large one at Gardabani. Tbilsresi Joint stock company owns and operates the 1800 MW Gardabani thermal power plant. Smaller hydro power stations have been sold or given on lease to the private sector. Sakenergo became the transmission and load dispatch company and most of the distribution enterprises became municipally owned enterprises. The key expectation in decentralizing power distribution to municipal levels was that the popularly elected municipal politicians would be closer to the people and be effective in improving collections. Sakenergo acts as the sole purchaser of power from the generating companies and seller of power to the distribution companies. It also sells some power directly to a few large consumers.

E. Status of the Payment Situation

14.   As a result of the various steps taken, collection performance started improving slowly and reached the level of 57% for 1996 and 68% in 1997 compared the level of 20% in 1995. consumer category wise collection performance for 1996 and 1997 is summarized in Table 2 below.

Table 2: Collection Performance at the Distribution Level
(Amounts in Lari Million)

Category	1996				1997			
	Share in Gwh Sales (%)	Amount Billed	Amount Collected	Share of Collections (%)	Share in Gwh sales (%)	Amount Billed	Amount Collected	Share of Collections (%)
Households	57.3	57.1	15.2	27	57.2	87.2	33.8	39
Industry	22.5	40.6	33.8	83	23.0	43.1	50.0	116
Government Budget Entities	7.5	14.7	11.4	78	5.4	10.5	10.3	99
Commercial	12.7	24.9	17.6	71	14.4	26.6	20.2	76
Total	100.0	137.3	78.1	57	100.0	167.4	114.3	68

Source: WB Internal Documents

Note: Collections over 100 % includes payment of arrears. Also collections include 20% VAT

While the collections at the level of distribution companies improved, payments by distribution companies to Sakenergo lagged behind considerably. Thus collections by Sakenergo from them amounted only to 43.3% in 1996 and 53% in 1997 as can be seen from Table 3 below.

Table 3: Collections at the Level of Sakenergo
(Amounts in Lari million)

Item	1996				1997			
	Gwh	Amount Billed	Amount Collected	Share of collection (%)	Gwh	Amount Billed	Amount Collected	Share of Collection (%)
Total Sales	4859	121.4	63.73	52.5	4750	146.4	102.5	70
Sales to Distribution Companies	4158	96.4	41.73	43.3	3999	115.1	61.2	53
Sales to Direct Consumers	701	25.0	21.99	88.0	751	31.3	41.3	132

Source: WB Internal Documents

Collections of Sakenergo improved to 70% in 1997 largely on account of the direct consumers paying their dues in full along with arrears and in spite of the distribution companies dragging their feet. Debts to Sakenergo from the distribution companies and direct consumers are still large as can be seen from Table 4.

Table 4: Debts to Sakenergo
(Amount in Lari million)

Item	1996	1997
Distribution Companies	131.2	188.0
Direct Consumers	22.2	16.7
Total Debt	153.5	204.8

Source: WB Internal Documents

Debts to external suppliers of fuel and electricity exceeded $200 million as of 31 December 1997. Another major cause for worry in Georgia is the very low level of cash collections. The share of cash in total collections was only 37% in 1997, rest being barter (4%) and set off (59%) as can be seen from Table 5. Many observers believe that the cash portions of the collection may have been somewhat overstated and that actual cash may be lower. Unlike in other FSU states, barter plays a minor role in Georgia, perhaps because of the shrinking industrial sector and lack of natural resources. The use of barter is confined to the industrial consumers only. Also unlike in Russia, the distribution companies and Sakenergo, pass on the barter goods at the same value to generating companies or other creditors, who then arrange to reach them to the ultimate users of the bartered goods.

Table 5: Share of Cash in Collections at the Level of Sakenergo

Item	Cash (%)	Set Off (%)	Barter (%)
From Distribution Companies	45	5	50
From Direct Consumers	25	3	72
Total	37	4	59

Source: WB Internal Documents

15.   Set off or mutual cancellation of debts is widely practiced by central and local governments, as well as by industrial and commercial consumers. While the households do not use set off and prefer to pay cash, certain subsidy payments made by the governments on behalf of some households and privileged persons is invariably made by

set off. Widespread use of set off is a serious problem in Georgia, and the government issued a Decree in June 1998 permitting only direct set off between two parties and in effect prohibiting triangular and multiple chain set off. When enforced properly it may bring down the use of this mechanism, and greater transparency to the books of power entities.

F. Consumer Subsidies

16. The government appears to make two sets of subsidy payments to the power companies on behalf of residential consumers. The first relates to the 50% power price discounts given to 19 different categories of persons (war veterans, handicapped persons, personnel of the Ministries of Internal Affairs and State Security, Chernobyl victims, distinguished persons) and 100% discounts granted to War veterans over 70 years old and families of the casualties in the Abkhazia civil war. Sakenergo estimates that 20% of the total household consumption in the country could be attributed to such privileged consumption. In Telasi distribution company alone there are 45,000 persons entitled to 50% discounts and 13,000 entitled to 100% discount. Based on an annual average household power bill of $125, the cost of subsidy is estimated at $ 4.4 million in this distribution area alone. The subsidy entitlements have been notified by different ministries at different points of time, and because of the difficulties of finding which categories are subsidized by which budget line item of which ministry, the distribution companies are reported to be unable to claim the full reimbursement. In Telasi , the company had not been able to claim more than 20% of its dues on this account. Such payments, when made by governments, is always on the basis of set off against tax dues.

17. The second set of payments is an interim arrangement pending the proper identification of the poor families and the introduction of social protection measures for them. Under this the government has been paying the power companies a sum of Lari 3.0 million ($ 2.34 million) per month for the following categories of consumers:

(a)	Consumers in A&O provinces	60 kWh / month
(b)	934,000 pensioners	40 kWh or Lari 1.8 / month
(c)	Migrant refugees and settled refugees	40-60 kWh or Lari 1.8 to 3.8/m
(d)	360,000 employees of the government	60 kWh or Lari 2.5 /month
(e)	Consumption by government budget entities	Lari 0.3 to 0.5 million / month

These payments are effected regularly, but always by way of tax set off. In view of the tendency of the distribution companies to delay payments to Sakenergo, government has been transferring them direct to Sakenergo. Such payments are estimated to amount to 17% of the total distribution company payments to Sakenergo. Together these two subsidies amount to $ 44 million or less than 1% of the country's GDP in 1997.

G. Government Budget Entities

18.   As can be seen from Table 1, the dues from the government budget entities is not a major problem, unlike in the case of many other FSU states. The Government does maintain a special list of state enterprises to which power supply can not be cut off for non-payment, but by and large no arbitrary additions are made to it. These are estimated

to consume 5 to 6% of the total power consumption in the country. For the government budget entities, the government has established consumption limits and on that basis transfers every month Lari 300,000 to 500,000 a month to power companies. Thus accounts receivable is generally under control. However the GBEs do often exceed their limits of consumption, presenting a problem to the utility. Government tries to deal with this through administrative sanctions and disciplinary action against heads of such GBEs. Clearly, this is an interim solution and the government must soon institute more effective budgeting and budget control measures and allow the GBEs to be cut off for payment defaults. There is no substitute to market place discipline.

H. Steps to Check Theft and Improve Collections

19.   The enactment of the new electricity law enabling disconnection for payment defaults and prosecution for power theft is a major advance. Still this could be effective only when the utilities improve the technical features of the distribution system to enable the disconnection of individual consumers. A range of pilot projects have been undertaken under donor assistance and they have highlighted the importance and efficacy of measures such as: (a) relocating meters outside the apartments in locked boxes; (b) checking and re-calibrating meters at periodic intervals and replacing defective meters; (c) introduction of intermediate metering such as metering the feeders and the apartment blocks as a whole; (d) rehabilitation of distribution transformers and substations; and (e) creating capability to disconnect individual consumers and enforcing strictly the disconnection policy for non-payment. Based on these a Presidential Decree was issued in February 1998 requiring the relocation of all meters outside the apartments. The pilot project in Rustavi incorporating these and other measures such as computerized consumer accounting and dispatch of power through feeders based on the payment performance of clients connected to the feeder (in the context of power shortage) resulted in dramatic improvements in collections from 20% to 80% in just two or three months and power supply could be restored to the level of 22 hours per day. The replication of these measures in all other areas needs a significant amount of new investment.

20.   The functions of meter reading, billing and collection had been tried in many different ways. The distribution companies engaged inspectors and controllers on a three month contract and paid them commissions based on collections. When this did not work, the entire work was outsourced to the so called "distributors" (they are like the resellers in other FSU states). In 1996, this was widely practiced covering for example 50% of sales in Telasi area. Their performance turned out to be the worst among all category of consumers (15% collection rate) and also raised questions regarding the transparency of the transactions. They collected the dues but simply did not pass them on to the power companies. By November 1997 this was abandoned and utilities hired inspectors and controllers on a full time basis and paid them remuneration based on collection performance. Still the situation is far from satisfactory. The meter reader also prepares and serves the bill and collects the cash in person from the residential customers and deposits them in the Bank to the account of the power company. The Banks then are to transfer 70% of the funds to Sakenergo and leave 30% in the accounts of distribution company. The procedures are leak prone and cash handling does not conform standard commercial practices. There is reason to believe that vested interests are emerging around such leaks. A Presidential Decree issued in April 1998, has the effect of requiring the

consumers to pay their electricity bills only in the banks or post offices. When properly enforced, this should go a long way in preventing leaks and enforcing disconnection for non-payment without any hesitation.

21.   Two other experiments going on in Georgia are worth taking note of. First, the use of electronic prepaid meters is being experimented in a neighborhood in Tiblisi with 1500 customers. The meters are being provided by Energia, an Israeli-Georgian joint venture, which buys power from Telasi Distribution Company at a tariff of 3.15 tetri/kWh (Cents 2.46/kWwh) and sells it to customers at the National Electricity Regulation determined end user price of 4.5 tetri/kWh (Cents 3.52/kwh). Energia guarantees payment for all power purchased and collects revenue from customers in the form of prepayment. This could be a very attractive solution to overcome the problems of leakage in collections from residential customers. The effectiveness of this option in Georgian setting is yet to be evaluated. Second, Telasi Distribution Company has an agreement with Gldanienergo 96, valid through the end of 1998, under which Gldani buys power from Sakenergo and uses Telasi network to supply it to its consumers. Telasi receives a transit fee and is obliged to provide well maintained "wire services" for this contract. This is the first case of an energy merchant entering the business. The effectiveness of this also remain to be evaluated.

I. The Decentralization Experience

22.   The ostensible reason for decentralization of power distribution to municipal level was the expectation that municipalities being closer to the consumers would be able to collect the charges for power more efficiently. Collections did improve after the decentralization, but many believe that the correlation between the two is spurious. It is generally believed that collections improved because of the intensive action initiated by government (often as a result of the Bank's suggestions) and not because of the municipalization. However under the municipal ownership, the collected money did not flow upwards to Sakenergo and generating companies. Sakenergo has the power to disconnect distribution companies for payment default, but that is not a practical option as it will penalize a large number of paying customers. Sakenergo files complaints in courts against delinquent distribution companies for arrears and obtains orders to confiscate funds flowing into the accounts of such companies. As in other FSU states, it evokes the response of the distribution companies avoiding flow of cash into their accounts, through increased non-cash transactions. A special commission of the Ministry of Internal Affairs was created (financed by fees collected from distribution companies) to conduct, in cooperation with Sakenergo, routine audits of the accounts of distribution companies. Based on such audits, Sakenergo repossessed the meter reading, billing and collection functions from Kutaisi distribution company.. By now the government is disillusioned with the municipalization of the power distribution, and understands that 66 distribution companies are too many to sell 5000 Gwh of power to 1.2 million consumers and that they essentially lack economies of scale. The government is in the process of consolidating them into four large viable entities and effectively privatizing them to strategic investors. This is being pursued with Merril Lynch as financial advisor. Ten % of the shares will go to the staff of these companies and 51 to 75% will go the strategic investor and the rest will be auctioned

J. Approach to Tariffs

23.   The Georgian case clearly highlighted the need to improve reliability of supply to improve collections. A key to maintain reliable supply is to keep the power sector viable through the adoption of tariffs which recover the cost of supply. While this still remains a goal to be achieved in Georgia, the tariffs in the last three years have moved closer to costs of supply. The recent tariff changes for residential, industrial and commercial consumers is summarized below.

Table 6: Tariff Changes in Power Sector
(US Cents/kWh)

Period	Industries	Commercial	Households
1996	3.52	3.52	1.95
January-July 1997	3.52	3.52	2.58
Since July 1997	3.52	3.52	3.52

Source: WB Internal Documents

The tariff for households is due for revision to the level of Cents 4.69 in the course of 1998[45]. Thus the tariffs are moving in the right direction and the internal cross subsidy is being reduced. Since August 1997, the tariff at the level of generation is at an average of Cents 1.52 / kWh, and Sakenergo sells to the distribution companies and direct consumers at a price range of Cents 2.42 to 2.58. Retail tariff for all classes of consumers is at Cents 3.52 / kWh. A National Electricity Regulatory Commission with an experienced Chairman and a complement of 17 professional staff (expected to go up to 50) has been functioning since July 1997 and is likely to evolve into an independent and competent organization.

K. Areas for Future Reform and Follow Up

24.   To sustain the progress achieved and to fully overcome the payment problems, Georgia needs to make its power sector commercialization program much more aggressive and focus on the following areas:

- Achieve political normalcy in Abkhazia and South Ossetia provinces, as the present non-recovery of dues from the consumers there is a major problem.
- Get rid of the special list of enterprises to which power supply can not be cut off and subject them as well as all GBEs to the discipline of disconnection for non-payment.
- Eliminate the two sets of consumer subsidies and replace it with targeted social protection for the poor households.
- Desist from political interference at all levels in the disconnection decisions.
- Strengthen the independence and competence of NERC and its stature and ability to resolve payment disputes among licensees using its power to revoke licenses for non-compliance.
- Introduce incentive and punitive mechanisms against theft of power.

---

[45] This revision has already taken place. Currently the residential tariff is 6 tetri / kWh equivalent to about US cents 4.4 at the exchange rate of US$1= 1.35 Lari

- On a priority basis, privatize to strategic investors, the four distribution companies[46].
- With multilateral and bilateral assistance rehabilitate on a priority basis key power facilities to improve reliability of supply.

REFERENCES

1. Georgia Power Rehabilitation Project- SAR, May 1997
2. Georgia Country Assistance Strategy Report, September 1997
3. Information Memorandum on Telasi Distribution Company
4. Preliminary Assessment of Distribution Sector for Privatization- Hagler Bailly Report, November 1997
5. Notes of Ms. Nina Bubnova on Collections in Georgia
6. BTORS of Bank Missions to Georgia- 1997 and 1998

---

[46] Telasi, the largest among the distribution companies, has been privatized to AES Silk Road towards the end of 1998.

THE RUSSIAN CASE STUDY

A. Economic Background

1.   There has been a continuous decline in the GDP of Russia since the break-up of the Soviet Union. During the period 1989-1996, GDP declined by 43% and 1997 was the first year in which a growth of 0.8% was believed to have been registered. However the developments of the second half of 1998 have sent the economy back to its declining trend. Annual inflation rose to a high of 2,500% in 1992 and came down to 11% in 1997. Unemployment rose to a high level of about 10% by 1997. The fiscal deficit was in the range of 7.5 to 8.5 % of GDP even during 1996-97. Control of inflation would appear to have been achieved more by issuing high interest rate treasury bills (GKOs), than by raising additional resources by way of tax revenues. Money supply had been curtailed sharply to fight inflation and the volume of broad money (M2) came down from 70% of GDP in 1990 to about 13-14 % range in 1996-97[47]. External trade had been the only encouraging factor, and current account had been moderately on the surplus side in the recent years. The value of Ruble had fallen from 1.7 Ruble to 6,000 Rubles to a dollar during 1990-1997. The country with a population of about 148 million and a per capita GDP of about $3,000 in 1997 (which had suffered an economic collapse, the depth and duration of which is the longest among all the countries under consideration) is again headed in 1998 towards further deteriorating circumstances.

B. Impact on Power Sector

2.   The economic downturn had its inevitable impact on the power sector of the country. The dissolution of the Soviet Union split the old Unified Energy System and made the truncated Russian power system some what unbalanced in certain areas. Still the Russian power system is one of the largest in the world. It has a total installed capacity of 216 GW (including 21 GW of obsolete units to be retired), 70% of which is thermal, 20% hydro and 10% nuclear. The system has over 2.5 million kms of transmission lines of which 30,000 kms are at 500 kV, 750 kV and 1150 kV. On account of the age of the generating units and transmission constraints, only a capacity of about 180 GW is considered reliable. The peak demand in 1997 was estimated at only 134 GW and it is expected to recover to the 1990 level sometime in the second half of the next decade. The fall in the electricity demand was, however, at a lower rate than that of the GDP. During 1990-1997, overall electricity consumption fell from 1074 TWh to 813 TWh or by 24%, while electricity consumption by industries fell by 34%. The share of industries in the total consumption fell from 57 % to about 51%, while the share of the households increased from 11% to about 29%[48]. As a consequence of the economic decline and the corrective actions to stabilize the economy, the sector institutions started accumulating arrears from the consumers, and in turn accumulated accounts payable to its suppliers, wage arrears to staff and tax arrears to government. One estimate places the total volume of economy- wide arrears at about $ 127 billion and that of the utilities sector at about 30% of this level. The existence of such a high level of inter-agency

---

[47] Compared with 43% in France, 35% in Poland and 30% in Mexico.

[48] Includes consumption by residences, residential areas and residential resellers.

arrears reduces government's tax receipts, widens fiscal deficits and impedes economic growth. Corporate tax receipts as a percentage of GDP in Russia is believed to have declined from 10% in 1993 to about 4% in 1997. The problem is further compounded by the disappearance of cash from the system, by every one trying to settle dues by barter, offsets or promissory notes. Thus in the Russian power sector, non-cash settlement of dues is even greater a problem than non-payment. Such a lack of liquidity in the system led to supply constraints in the midst of excess capacity, irrational dispatch of generation pushing up costs all around, maintenance back log, and worsening of system reliability. During 1996 the power system operated at frequencies lower than 49.8 cycles per second for about 20% of the time and load shedding was resorted to maintain frequency even at this level. In 1997 the system operated at standard frequency for about 98% of the time.

C. Sector Structure and Institutions

3.   As a result of the sector reorganization carried out in the early 1990s, RAO UES has been established as the apex holding company owning the high voltage transmission system, load dispatching facilities and (through subsidiaries) a substantial percentage of the large sized thermal and hydro generating units (about 46 GW). Rosenergoatom, a state owned company, owns 8 nuclear plants, while the nuclear plant at Leningrad is directly owned by the government. There are 72 regional electricity companies (known as AO Energos) which are vertically integrated power companies owning substantial generating capacities (over 110 GW), combined heat and power plants, transmission lines at 330 kV or lower, and the power and heat distribution systems. Government owns 100% of the shares in Rosenergoatom and 52.7% of the shares in RAO UES, which in turn owns 100% of the transmission and load dispatch facilities, 49 to 100% of the shares in generating companies and varying percentages of shares in the AO Energos.[49] Rest of the shares in RAO UES, generation subsidiaries and AO Energos are widely held (on the basis of mass privatization) by workers, managers and the public. Foreigners also hold some shares through portfolio investment, as many of these companies are listed in the Russian stock exchange and the shares are traded. About 30.7% of the shares of RAO UES are thus held by foreigners.

4.   In the absence of shareholding by any strategic investor with substantial stakes, the controlling interest in all the subsidiary generating companies and AO Energos remains with RAO UES, in which the controlling interest is that of the federal government. Thus despite corporatization and partial privatization of the sector, the earlier management culture persists and no major improvement in corporate governance appears to have taken place. As the largest shareholder, RAO UES nominates the chairmen and several directors of the board and the chief executive officers of AO Energos. At the federal government level, the Ministry of Fuels and Energy is responsible for the sector. Federal Energy Commission (FEC) at the federal level regulates the tariffs for the wholesale electricity supply and defines procedures for tariff setting at the end-user level. Regional Energy Commissions (REC) at the level of regions have the responsibility to regulate the

---

[49] RAO UES share holding is less than 49% in 7 energos, 49% in 14 energos, between 49% and 99% in 42 energos and 100% in 9 energos. In Tatenergo and Irkutskenergo, RAO UES has no shares at all, and all the shares appear to be held by the regional governments.

end-user tariffs following the procedures laid down by FEC[50]. The generating units owned by the generation subsidiaries of RAO UES and those owned by AO Energos with surplus capacity, supply electricity to the wholesale power market (FOREM), from which other AO Energos and large industrial consumers buy at wholesale prices determined by FEC. All the participants in the wholesale market except the atomic power plants of Rosenergoatom pay RAO UES a fee for the use of the transmission and dispatch facilities and associated grid services.

5.   Most of the AO Energos have a fully owned subsidiary called Energosbyt which performs the functions of metering and billing of all consumers, and collecting dues from the consumers who pay in cash or through bank transfer. Most Energos have also resellers (mostly owned by the municipalities) which retail electricity and heat to the end-users in their area. They are authorized to retain 20% of their collections for their use and maintenance of the distribution system. On an average, it is estimated that about 25% of the total electricity sales go through the resellers. In some regions, the percentage could be as high as 55%. In respect of heat sales, the proportions are much larger. The electricity companies are liable to pay VAT at 20% of the sales revenue and also a tax on the profits they make. In addition they are also believed to be liable to pay other minor taxes to the regional and local governments.

D. The Payment Problem

6.   The 72 AO Energos in Russia are grouped into seven zones and the collection performance (in respect of power and heat sales) for each zone as a percentage of billings during 1996 is given in Table 1 below:

Table 1: Collection Performance in the AO Energos in 1996.
(As a % of billing)

Zone	Total Collections	Cash Collection	Promissory Notes	Barter and Set-Off
Central	84	9	20	54
North Western	82	15	22	46
Volga	82	7	28	46
Ural	79	10	17	51
Siberia	86	10	15	60
Eastern	72	12	9	51
Southern	85	22	12	51

Source: WB Internal Documents

The collection performance as a percentage of billing varied from a low of 72 in the Eastern Zone (with the highest average tariff US Cents 4.95 / kwh) to a high of 86 in the Siberian Zone (with the lowest average tariff at US cents 2.05 / kwh). As can be seen from Table 1, collection in cash (7 to 22%)was quite low compared to non-cash collection (78 to 93%) by way of promissory notes, barter and set off. Collection performance for the first eight months of 1998 are summarized in Table 2. For all the 72 AO Energos during this period, sales of power and heat amounted to 138.5 billion rubles

---

[50] Municipally owned electricity and heat supply systems are regulated by the municipalities themselves and not by the RECs.

and collections were at 115.7 billion rubles or 84% of the billings. Collections were predominantly by way of barter (58%) followed by cash (15%), offsets (6%) and promissory notes (5%)[51]. Cash collection performance in Mosenergo (in the Moscow area) at 47% pushed up the average of the central zone to 25%, but for the country as a whole, however, there was no special improvement. The share of the promissory notes appears to be declining while that of the barter is rising.

Table 2: Collection Performance of AO Energos in January-August 1998
(As a % of Billings)

Zone	Total Collections	Share of Cash	Share of Promissory Notes	Share of Set-Off	Share of Barter
Central	84	25	4	7	48
North Western	84	14	6	4	60
Volga	77	7	9	4	57
Ural	86	8	8	5	65
Siberian	86	16	neg	7	63
Eastern	79	14	4	6	55
Southern	84	14	3	7	60
Total for Russia	84	15	5	6	58

Source: WB Internal Documents

7.   Arrears from power and heat consumers of the 72 AO Energos was estimated to have risen from 43 trillion rubles in 1995 to 79 trillion rubles ($13.5 billion) by the end of 1996, and to 102 trillion rubles ($ 17 billion) by the end of 1997. The shares of the various categories of consumers in the total arrears, in comparison with their shares in the total consumption in 1997 is given in Table 3 below:

Table 3: Shares in Total Consumption and in Arrears of Consumer categories

Consumer Category	Share in Total Consumption in 1997 (%)	Share in Total Arrears at the End of 1997 (%)
Industry and Construction	56	37
Non-Industry	7	26
Residences	7	5
Wholesalers (Resellers)	19	19
Agriculture	7	9
Transport and Communication	4	4

Source: WB Internal Documents

As of September 1, 1998, the accounts receivable further rose to the level of 123.5 billion rubles[52]($20 billion) or approximately equal to 7.1 months sales. As can be seen from Table 4 below, the share of industries in the arrears was the highest at 36.4% followed by communal households at 19.3%. Looked at from a different perspective, the share of the arrears from wholesalers and resellers (most of which belong to the local administrations) was the highest at 21.5% followed by federal government budget entities (13.3%), and

---

[51] Expressed as a percentage of collections (rather than billings) the share of barter would be 69% followed by cash (18%), set off (7%), and promissory notes (6.5%).

[52] These are new rubles equivalent to 1000 old rubles.

regional and local government budget entities (11.5%). The arrears caused by the non-payment by government of compensation for tariff discounts appeared to be unexpectedly low at less than 1%.

Table 4: Analysis of Power and Heat Arrears of AO Energos by Consumer Categories as of September 1, 1998

Category	Arrears in Million Rubles	Percentage Share
Industry	44971	36.4
Agriculture and Forestry	10821	8.8
Transport and Communications	4413	3.5
Construction	1027	1.0
Communal Households	23840	19.3
Households	5219	4.2
Others	33253	27.0
Total	123545	100.0
Memo Items:		
Wholesalers and Resellers	26531	21.5
Federal GBEs	16403	13.3
Regional and Local GBEs	14146	11.5
Compensation for Tariff Discounts	837	0.7

Source: WB Internal Documents

The Annual Report of RAO UES for 1996 indicates that its accounts receivable from the AO Energos as of 31 December 1996 stood at 10.6 trillion rubles ($.1.77 billion) or equivalent to 14 months of energy sales. This was 60% higher than the level at the end of the previous year and compares with the level of 1.29 trillion rubles at the end of 1993. Recent information indicates that these have grown to the level of 12.225 billion rubles[53] (or equivalent to 13.5 months sales) as of September 1, 1998. Charges for the use of transmission and grid services payable to RAO UES by AO Energos amounted to 7,260 million rubles while collections were at about 50% or 3,658 million rubles during the first 8 months of 1998. Cash payments, which were at 14% during January- May rose to 21% during January-August 1998. Sales of 270 Twh or about 33% of total sales went through the wholesale power market or FOREM in 1997. Overall collection performance in FOREM was about 80%. Collection was highest from the central region at 85% and lowest from exports at 54%. Accounts receivable in FOREM rose by 1.5 times during 1997 and reached the level of 8 months sales equivalent. Cash payment was lowest in this segment of the market. Cash payment performance of buyers to the generating subsidiaries of RAO UES via the FOREM had traditionally been very low. Most of the large and efficient plants of these companies thus were so completely cash constrained that they could not procure fuel and pay wages to operate their units[54].

---

[53] These are new rubles equal to 1,000 old rubles.

[54] Thus the more efficient RAO UES units had plant load factors (40-43%) much lower than the highly inefficient smaller generating units (48-50%) of AO Energos. Such a perverse system of dispatch is believed to push up the system costs by over 20% of the variable costs or about $ 3 .0 to $ 5.0 billion annually, according to the estimates made by the Energy Research Institute in 1996. Even supply disruptions in the AO Energos in the Far eastern zone (such as Dalenergo) are attributed to the lack of fuels caused by the liquidity crunch.

8.   The problem has emerged in the last six or seven years and has spiraled to serious proportions in the last two years. The lack of liquidity on the part of power and heat companies, results in their accumulating arrears to their suppliers and arrears of tax payments to the federal and local governments, which in turn are unable to make adequate provision in the budgets for various government budget supported entities to pay in full for their power and space heating needs, especially in the context of the overriding need to contain fiscal deficits to control inflation and stabilize the economy. It has established a vicious cycle from which it is becoming increasingly difficult to escape. Though the problem of arrears and that of payment in kind seem to be economy wide covering a range of sectors, they are pronounced and acute in the energy sector. A recent estimate by RAO UES places the level of accounts receivable of the energy producers to be above 50% of the total accounts receivable in the entire industrial sector. RAO UES, with tax arrears amounting to 551.4 billion rubles (or $95m), was the 19th largest debtor to the federal budget after Lukoil, Avto Vaz, and Gazprom[55]. Though RAO UES managed to become current on tax payments by end 1997, the arrears from 19 AO Energos amounted to 4.57 trillion rubles (or $789 million) and that from the remaining 53 AO Energos was believed to be much larger.

E. Causes for Non-Payment

9.   Non-payment in the power and heat sectors is mostly from government budget entities and from insolvent industries-- the former because of inadequate budget provisions in the context of the overriding need to contain fiscal deficits to control inflation and stabilize the economy, and the latter because of contraction of GDP and loss of markets. RAO UES has estimated that as of September 1, 1998 arrears of federally funded budget entities to AO Energos was 13.3% and that from locally funded budget entities was 11.5%. Among the locally funded budget entities, those funded by the city budgets were the worst offenders, mainly for the reason that power and heat dues from them to the AO Energos were much larger than the tax dues from the AO Energos to the city.

10.   Federal and regional governments maintain a strategic list of consumers, the power and heat supply to which can not be disconnected by the energy entities, even when they chronically default in the payment of bills. This list generally includes the military industrial complex, key research institutes, communication services and other essential services. Through the influence of federal, regional and local politicians, a number of non-strategic and solvent industries also managed to get into this list, thereby severely limiting the ability of AO Energos to recover arrears by resorting to disconnection procedures. In pursuance of the reforms supported by SAL I of the Bank, the government pruned this list substantially in January 1997 retaining only the entities responsible for external and internal security. The federal government also made provisions in the 1997 budget for those retained in the list and committed to ensure that they will not have arrears in the future. The government also tried unsuccessfully to liquidate the past stock

---

[55] It must ,however, be noted that the arrears of federal government to RAO UES at 13 trillion rubles was
      2.5 times larger as of July 1, 1997.

of its debts by tax offsets. Subsequently in November 1997 a Presidential Decree was issued prohibiting the federal government from using any form of mutual off set including cash off set for clearing tax arrears and payment arrears with effect from January 1998, and recommending that regional governments do the same. The situation at the regional level , however, is not believed to have improved. Regional Governors are believed to enforce informally the old list and prevent reduction or discontinuance of supplies to any industry (even if it is not a government budget entity) favored by the local administrations. The prescribed procedures for reduction or disconnection of supply, mandate that AO Energos must inform the regional administration and the Ministry of Fuel and Energy at least one day prior to the proposed reduction or disconnection and this gives ample time to the regional officials to intervene in the matter. AO Energos themselves are not often very enthusiastic about cutting off supplies to major industrial customers and ruin their main market base, and tend to work out other arrangements hoping to liquidate arrears in phases. RAO UES reports that as of September 1, 1998, debts of government budget entities (covering federal, regional and municipal governments) to AO Energos and RAO UES amounted to 30.5 billion rubles ($ 5.0 billion).

11.   The nature of involvement of the regional and local officials in the power and heat sector is considered a major reason for the non-payment problem. Apart from their intervention in the reduction or disconnection of supplies to defaulting customers, they exercise considerable political influence over the AO Energos through the RECs. The chairmen and members of RECs are appointed by the Regional Governors and are on the payroll of the regional governments. The RECs have not yet emerged as independent regulatory bodies. The regional politicians tend to believe that until the local industries overcome their economic crisis, AO Energos should subsidize them, by continuing to supply power and heat even when they can not pay for them. Similarly the regional politicians also insist on the AO Energos purchasing their supplies from the local industries, even when the latter do not offer any price or quality advantages. The regional politicians also tend to oppose vigorously any proposal to reduce or phase out the subsidies for the power and heat consumers. RAO UES has the perception that regional administrations use the RECs (beholden to them) "to redistribute power company resources in favor of social programs and nonviable enterprises." Often RECs increase the rates for federal budget entities, while keeping them low for the regional ones. Compounding the problem is the ambiguity in the legal framework. Part 2 of the Civil Code and article 215.1 of the Criminal Code of the Russian Federation seem to create a conflict between the right of the energy supplier to enforce payment by disconnection for default and the public nature of the power supply arrangements[56]. Local officials tend to exploit these ambiguities and harass the utility officials who dare to disconnect.

12.   The behavior of the resellers is considered a major reason for the accumulation of arrears to the AO Energos. Their debts to AO Energos amounted to 27 billion rubles as of 1 September 1998 or 22 % of the total accounts receivable. The customer base for the

---

[56] A draft of new energy supply rules, currently under review by the Russian Government seeks to remove these conflicts or ambiguities. However, it would also be necessary to amend the provisions of the Civil Code and the Criminal Code.

resellers consists mostly of residential consumers other small non-industrial consumers who tend to pay their bills regularly and in cash. The resellers (many owned by the municipalities) collect the cash, but do not pass them on fully to AO Energos. They retain more than their share of 20%, thereby leading to the accumulation of arrears at the level of the AO Energos. In Novosibirskenergo, for example, the resellers account for 15.6% of the power sales and 57% of the heat sales, but pay to the energo only for 71% of the power and 51% of the heat payments received by them. In many regions (such as in Komi), the resellers and municipal systems are being eliminated, by the AO Energo taking over their systems, since their accumulated debt exceed the book value of their assets. In other regions, AO Energos have started collecting dues from the customers directly, and paying to the resellers their 20% commission for the maintenance of the system. RAO UES advocates the policy of eliminating the resellers altogether. The total number of resellers has come down from 1343 (as of January 1, 1998) to 1256 (as of October 1, 1998).

13.   The past approach of the government towards tariffs involving significant cross subsidization of residential consumers by industrial consumers is believed to have imposed heavy burdens on the industry, making them noncompetitive and causing them to default in payments[57]. The Federal Energy Commission is conscious of this and has declared a policy of eliminating this cross subsidy gradually and is urging the RECs to move in this direction. Resolution 1231 dated September 26, 1997 of the Federal Government declares its intention to eliminate this kind of cross subsidy by the year 2000. The situation in 1996, represented in Table 5 below indicates that a great deal of corrective action is required.

Table 5: Power Tariffs Prevailing in Russia in 1996
(US Cents/ kWh)

Zone	Average Tariff	Industries > 750 kW	Industries < 750 kW	Households
Central	4.33	5.23	6.71	1.33
North West	3.78	4.51	5.79	1.33
Volga	3.67	4.96	5.17	0.71
Ural	3.75	4.37	5.07	1.21
Siberia	2.05	2.05	3.90	1.11
Eastern	4.95	6.79	9.66	2.63
Southern	4.41	6.92	7.02	1.32

Source: WB Internal Documents

Some progress has been achieved in 1997 and the tariffs as of January 1, 1998 indicate that the overall average tariff /kWh for the country has moved up to US Cents 4.39 (varying from 2.60 Cents to 6.58 Cents among the zones), that the industrial tariffs are around 7 to 9 Cents, while the residential tariffs moved up to be around 3 cents. Nearly a third of the AO Energos now have increasing block tariffs for households, and 15 AO Energos have tariffs differentiated by voltage levels. Nonetheless the cross subsidization seems to have been addressed only marginally. Progress in certain regions such as Komi,

---

[57] Such cross subsidization is also believed to cause residential consumers to account for 10 to 20% of the incremental demand.

where the residential tariffs will, by the end of the year, be actually be higher than industrial tariffs, is remarkable.

14.   There is a wide range of federally mandated subsidies in respect of heat and power to residential consumers, and these are payable to the energy companies by the regional and municipal governments from out of the block grants they receive from federal government. A wide range of privileged residential consumers are entitled to 50% discounts on their power bills; they include pensioners, blood donors, employees of the Ministry of Interior (including judges and policemen), employees of the city governments, victims of Chernobyl accident etc. In many regions over 50% of the residential consumers qualify for such discounts. Also the tariff for heat supply for households are kept at levels lower than 50% of the cost of supply, resulting in the subsidies payable to heat companies becoming substantial On account of the fiscal constraints, full amounts of the subsidy are not provided in the budgets and, in any case, even the partial provisions are diverted for other uses by regional and city governments and do not reach the AO Energos, since the block grants from federal government do not earmark the funds for such subsidies. This is considered an important source of liquidity constraint for the AO Energos.

F. Modes of Payment in Kind

15.   In Russia, payment of the power and heat bills in kind rather than cash has emerged as a more serious problem than the non-payment of bills. Non-cash payment methods include: (a) mutual settlement of dues, (b) payment by barter, (c) payment by allocation of shares and (c) payment by promissory notes known as 'vexels'. The adjustment of the fuel bills of the power and heat companies against the power and heat arrears from the fuel suppliers takes place often. Mutual settlement of dues (offsets) takes place in a triangular fashion, when the power and heat dues from government budget entities (such as schools, hospitals, research centers, military industrial complex etc.) are adjusted against the taxes payable by the Energos to the government. This takes place periodically at the federal, regional and city levels. When the tax dues are smaller than the power and heat arrears from the respective budget entities (as is the case in respect of cities) the effectiveness of this mechanism is limited. Under the barter system, supplies needed by the utility are received as barter payment for the energy or heat supplied. It may also involve payment by other types of goods (not needed for the utility) for the disposal of which intermediaries are made use of. Occasionally industries unable to pay cash for their power and heat consumption allocate equity shares in their company to the utility to settle their arrears. Promissory notes are accepted at their full face value as cash equivalents or at varying levels of discount depending on the financial condition /liquidity of the issuer.

G. Causes for Payment in Kind

16.   Though the resort to such non-cash mechanisms originated initially in the desire of the utilities to recover something, rather than nothing, from the defaulting consumers (especially in the context of constraints in the exercise of their option to curtail or cease electricity or heat supplies), the sharp increase in the recent years in such transactions has been attributed mainly to: (a) the propensity of the utilities to evade or avoid taxes based on cash turn over such as VAT; (b) the propensity of the managers of utilities for personal enrichment through the use of such mechanisms as barter and vexels; (c) mass privatization of the utilities resulting in a lack of corporate governance driven by profit maximization motive of any strategic investor; (d) inadequate management and financial controls, and (e) institutional structures and mechanisms which inhibit, either by default or (more often) by design, the flow of cash to the utility accounts from even the customers who pay in cash.

17.   Taxes such as VAT are collected on a cash basis, rather than on an accrual basis. Further, in the context of corporate and other tax arrears, the bank accounts of Energos are frozen and cash going into such accounts are automatically garnished by the Treasury towards tax arrears. Anecdotal evidence suggests that Energos minimize the flow of cash into their account, and keep the minimum cash needed for wages etc. in the accounts of Energosbyts and to collect the balance through barter or vexels even when the customer is willing to pay in cash. Thus the desire for tax avoidance seems to drive non-cash transactions.

18.   Barter transactions are perceived to lack transparency, enable considerable overvaluation and undervaluation of the bartered goods and lead to a significant level of under-the-table profits. When in 1997 RAO UES offered on an experimental basis a 30% discount on the power and heat bills for those who pay in cash, it found that none came forward to make use of the offer. The managers of the utilities seem to skim off the profits from barter transactions through an intermediary enterprise to handle all such transactions. The intermediary collects cash or cash equivalents from the customers , uses this cash to purchase goods and services needed for the utility at cash prices, and passes them on to the utility at barter prices which are inflated by 30% to 50%. Because of this potential for private gain at the expense of the organization, the share of barter in total sales transactions in Russian economy is believed to have increased from 17% in 1994 to 42% in 1997 despite a relatively better level of stabilization of the economy, improvement in the level of money supply and availability of credit[58] than in previous years.

19.   Vexels or promissory notes have come in handy to provide a more convenient form of multiple barter transactions[59] avoiding the cumbersome need for the transportation and

---

[58] The use of barter was highest in the intermediate goods sector at 55%. By December 1997 the share of barter transactions in the total sales in the industrial sector rose to 47%.

[59] It is reported, for example, that Novosibirskenergo at one time used 160 intermediaries to purchase fuel from 50 sources based on multiple barters.

storage of goods[60]. Energy enterprises accept vexels from their customers, and in turn provide these vexels to a lending enterprise in return for goods and services. The lending enterprise redeems the vexels from the customers who issued them and completes the cycle. The cash thus obtained by the lending intermediary is used to purchase goods and services at cash prices and supply them to the energy enterprise at an inflated price mainly as a function of the face value of the vexel and its secondary market value, which could be as low as 70 to 30% of the face value. Energy enterprises also issue vexels of their own, which could be used to pay for the consumption of energy by specified consumers at face value and consumption by others at negotiated values. By resorting to the mechanisms of barter and vexels, the energy companies effectively minimize the flow of cash resulting in tax avoidance and in many cases private gains at the expense of the company.

H. Possible Corrective Actions

20.   Since July 1997, RAO UES has announced a policy of accepting cash payments only and eliminating the practice of acceptance of payments by barter, promissory notes and mutual settlements. Improvements in its cash collection so far reported have been modest, since existing barter arrangements have to be respected. Nonetheless improvements in its cash collection enabled it to become current on tax payments by end 1997. It has also announced that industrial customers who clear their arrears and pay in cash for the consumption in advance would be given significant price discounts. However the problem requires a broader array of corrective actions at various levels.

21.   While the overall average price per kWh is low compared to those prevailing in other European countries, the tariff for the industrial consumers is high as they have to subsidize heavily the residential consumers. Tariff reform to correct the structure of tariffs to be in line with the cost of supply to different classes of consumers (best differentiated on the basis of voltage of supply) is overdue and needs to be pursued by FEC and RECs vigorously. The Bank's efforts to strengthen the hands of FEC and REC and to make them competent and independent needs to be kept up through suitably designed institutional support projects. RAO UES has identified the incompatibility of the tariff mechanism as it is being adopted for sales from the wholesale market to the AO Energos, with ease of clearing payments satisfactorily. The need for reform in this area should be reviewed and pursued.

22.   The   federally mandated extensive subsidies for a wide range of residential consumers of power and heat (see paragraph 13) is inefficient and should be carefully reviewed to eliminate those relating to various kinds of government staff, blood donors, pensioners and the like. They are best compensated directly by cash and not by giving them subsidized power or heat. The needs of the poorer sections of the public is best taken care of through an adequate social security safety network, rather than by giving them subsidized heat and power. A reform of this kind is difficult but necessary, if the energy entities are to be relieved of the burden placed on them arising from the

---

[60] The stock of vexels of all kinds in circulation in spring 1997 has been estimated to be in the range of 200 to 500 trillion rubles ($33-82 billion) or 7.5% to 18.5% of the GDP.

inadequate provisions for subsidies in the federal budgets and the high-jacking of them by regional and local governments. The Government has directed means tested income transfers by municipalities for families with expenditure exceeding 15% of the gross money income of the households on energy and rail transportation. There could be a case to tax electricity and use the proceeds to fund this means tested income transfer. The electricity prices are low because of the understatement of the capital component and taxing electricity may be justified to capture the rent. These efforts deserve donor support and encouragement. Meanwhile the block grants from the federal budget to regional and municipal budgets must earmark the funds destined for the energy companies as subsidy payments and prevent their diversion for other purposes. The budget law must also specify the timing, frequency and mode of payment of these subsidies to energy entities by the regional and local governments.

23.   Interference by the regional and local political executives on behalf of defaulting consumers should be eliminated, *inter alia*, by removing the need for Energos to give prior notice to the regional and local officials while curtailing or discontinuing supplies to defaulting consumers. Procedures for reducing or disconnecting supplies for payment default need to be simplified in line with the practices in market economies and made much less time consuming and cumbersome. Also the RECs should be made independent of the regional administrations by shifting the power to appoint chairmen and members from the regional government to FEC. FEC and the RECs should have independent sources of funds of their own (outside the federal and regional government budgets) such as the filing fees, license fees and perhaps a small charge from each energy company based on its sales volume. Some progress is being made in this regard.

24.   RAO UES is making efforts to move the FEC to issue directives enabling the elimination of resellers, and transfer of their consumer accounts to Energosbyts should Energos find it cost effective. In many regions at present, the regional and local politicians thwart any such move both directly and through RECs over which they have dominance. The experience with resellers in most countries had not been happy. Should it be found necessary to retain resellers in any area, because of the size and economies of scale, then they should be subject direct regulation by RECs as a distributing agency. They should also be made a corporate entity operating with their own books and accounts outside of those of the municipalities[61].

25.   Under the reform program covered by the first Structural Adjustment Loan (SAL I) of the World Bank, the federal and regional governments were expected to give up the practice of periodic adjustment of tax dues from energy entities against the power and heat arrears from government budget entities. The practice, however, persists at the regional and local levels. In this context there is a greater need under the SALs and IMF programs to ensure that budgets provide adequate and earmarked provisions for the power and heating needs of all the budget entities, prevent line item fungibility in this respect and devise financial control methods for the orderly flow of these funds to the

---

[61] In Novosibirskenergo resellers accounts have been transferred to the Energosbyt. The consumers now pay their dues in the State Savings Bank, which retains 3% for its own service charge, pays 20% to the reseller for the maintenance of the system and remits the balance to the account of the energo.

heat and power companies against their bills. RAO UES plan of action envisages that AO Energos at the regional level and municipal levels and RAO at the federal level work with the budget departments at the time of budget formulation to ensure adequate funding for the energy consumption of the budget entities and later work with the budget departments to monitor payments for consumption[62]. This needs to be supported. In the light of high interest rates still prevailing in Russia, price discounts by the energy entities could be considered for advance (annual or quarterly) payments in cash. Correspondingly, delayed payments should be subject to penal interest rates. Presidential Decree 889 issued on 25 July 1998 allowed industrial and budget consumers a 50% discount in prices for the power purchased by them from FOREM, if they paid 100% cash for 100% of their monthly consumption, subject to the condition that in any case the price should not be lower than the cost of power generation and transmission. In view of the low level of the prevailing tariffs, it is doubtful whether 50% of the tariff could really cover the true cost of generation and transmission. This needs to be examined carefully. Regarding the stock of past debts, government's plan of securitizing a portion of them through the issue of government bonds needs to be pursued.

26.   Under reform program covered by the second SAL, the government has agreed to carry out tax reforms and ensure more efficient tax collection. In order to eliminate the tax avoidance related incentives for non-cash transactions, accrual accounting methods should be adopted and VAT should be based on accrued sales (and not based on cash sales)[63] and corporate tax based on accrual accounting and appropriate provisions for bad debt. While tax collection should be rigorous, extensive freezing of bank accounts (especially the transit accounts) should perhaps be avoided, as it seems to drive the companies away from cash transactions and bank accounts. This aspect should be carefully reviewed under the IMF programs and SALs.

27.   The government has agreed with the Bank to move towards a set of GAAP conforming to IAS and reach a uniform system of accounts and audit certification by the year 2000. and to enforce independent audit of all enterprises from 1999 onwards. As a part of GAAP, the institution of chartered accountants should be helped to evolve standard methods of valuing non-cash transactions (such as barter and vexels) and the audits of energy entities must be required to focus specifically on the propriety of these transactions and the appropriateness of the related valuations. The auditors must be required to comment specifically on these aspects, both in their audit certificates and in the long form audit. The Federal Commission for Securities Market must ensure that the disclosure requirements for the listed companies (most energy entities are listed) include specifically details of the share of non-cash transactions, methods of valuation and related audit comments and certificates.

---

[62] Some progress has been made in this regard in 1998. The energy consumption by the Government and Government funded agencies is believed to have been reduced by 23%.

[63] Notifications issued in mid 1998, were turned down by the Constitutional Court and the related laws need amendment by Federal Duma.

28.   Under the IMF programs and SALs, it would be worthwhile to carry out a thorough review of the various types of vexel related transactions, the laws and regulations governing them and examine whether the regulations could be improved in the light of experience in other western countries to prevent abuse of these instruments[64]. This work may have to be undertaken by the CBR with consultant assistance. This will be in support of the Government's Resolution 1081 of 1997 to develop an action plan to strengthen control over barter transactions and the use of promissory notes (vexels) and money substitutes.

29.   The corporate problem of the managers of energy entities privately enriching themselves through barter and vexel based transactions could be mitigated by the accounts and audit related improvements mentioned above. More importantly it needs to be recognized as a major corporate discipline problem and handled through detection, dismissal of the erring managers and dismantling of arrangements with suspect intermediaries. RAO UES has controlling shareholding in Energos and appoints their chairmen and the chief executive officers and several directors on their boards. With a determined effort on its part, it should be possible for it to contain the problem in Energos. However, given its shareholding structure, it is open to question whether the apex company itself would have the motivation to pursue such efforts wholeheartedly. The privatization of RAO UES through mass privatization program, has left the controlling interest with the state and not with any qualified strategic investor with a clear responsibility for the financial performance of the company and an ability to exercise sufficient corporate governance, appropriate fiscal management and proper financial controls on behalf of the shareholders. Such an improvement is still possible. The government could retain a single golden share and sell the rest of the shares to one or more qualified strategic investors.

30.   Given the size and diversity of the country and its power systems, the relationship among the regions and the federal government, one wonders whether the top down approach of sector reorganization with an apex holding company is a practical solution. Perhaps the reorganization by the government could have taken the route of allowing the emergence of strong privately owned generating companies and Energos run by strategic investors at the regional level and the evolution of a cooperatively owned national grid and dispatching facilities as a mechanism enabling the generators and Energos to maximize their business and profits under the watchful refereeing by FEC. The creation of the National Energy Market in which the generating companies could directly conclude sales contracts with customers willing to clear their arrears and pay in advance for purchases in cash[65] and the proposals to further privatize Energos to strategic investors in convenient phases gives room for the hope that a more suitable sector structure would emerge in the medium term.

---

[64] Widespread use of vexels and similar instruments can be gauged from the fact that the use of vexels accounted for 50% of the consolidated revenues and 39% of the expenditure in the regional and local government budgets.

[65] This arrangement is growing and should be welcomed. However its practice of giving 35% price discount for advance cash payment is a troubling aspect which needs to reviewed carefully. The price should be left to be negotiated freely between the generator and the buyer.

I. Recent Initiatives

31.   Some of the recent initiatives which give room for cautious optimism include: (a) steps taken by RAO UES to strengthen financial controls such as the consolidation of the several dozens of its accounts in several commercial banks into a master account with Sberbank of Russian Federation, creation of a treasury department to control cash flows and to effect centralized control of the flow of funds both in RAO UES and in its regional divisions; (b) disconnection of supplies by the Central Dispatch Unit of RAO UES to the extent of 7 to 10 Gwh to the non-paying consumers in many zones, and reducing supplies to 9 AO Energos with large debts to RAO UES; (c) issue of Resolution #1 dated January 5, 1998 and Resolution # 789 dated July 17.1998 of the federal government seeking to simplify and streamline disconnection procedures and to enable curtailment of power supplies to "technological emergency minimum level" to a list of GBEs,(which had till then remained exempt from disconnection for payment default) if they delayed payment by more than two months, and to enable the termination of even the curtailed level of supply if they further continued to default; (d) issue of Resolution #5 dated January 5, 1998 which established energy consumption limits to federal GBEs and sought to provide earmarked line item funds in the budget of 1998 to pay for them (GBE arrears for 1997 and earlier years were sought to be restructured and partly offset against tax arrears of RAO UES and fuel suppliers); (e) issue of Resolution # 555 dated June 3,1998 providing guidelines to develop energy consumption limits for Regional GBEs (this is yet to be implemented); and (f) issue of orders by the federal government seeking to enhance the scrutiny of the four largest tax debtors to the government, namely, RAO UES, Gazprom, Aerofloat, and Railroads for increased transparency and elimination of suspect intermediaries who siphon off cash (this resolution also calls for IAS style consolidation of the accounts of all subsidiaries to enable greater scrutiny by government).

J. Lessons from the Russian Case

32.   The Russian case study brings home the point that the payment problem in Russia is largely a function of corporate indiscipline, and partly a function of the tax laws and procedures (requiring urgent reform) and the absence of regulatory oversight of barter and vexel based transactions. The roots of the primary cause are to be found in the methods of privatization used and the approach to sector reorganization adopted. Also in the transition economies, politicians and people need to be disabused of the notions that power and heat supply is a "public good" to which everybody is entitled and that energy entities are the vehicles to keep afloat the insolvent industries to protect local jobs. Suitable public awareness campaigns should be initiated to enable politicians and the people to understand that supply of power and heat is a commercial service to be obtained only upon payment of the agreed price.

REFERENCES

1. President's Report and Recommendation: SAL II, November 1997
2. Country Assistance Strategy for Russia, May 1997
3. Technical Annex, Russian Federation Electricity Sector Reform Support Project, May 1997
4. Wilson, James. F., and Igor S. Sorokin, Electric Power Sector: Diagnostic Review, Policy Positions and Recommendations for Future Work, December 1994
5. Bagratian, Hrant and Emine Gurgen, Payment arrears in the Gas and electric Power Sectors of Russian Federation and Ukraine, September 1997
6. Anderson, Robert E, Russian Power Sector Reform: Old Wine in New Bottles? October 1997
7. Bull, Greta, Collection Issues at Energo Level, March 1998
8. Hagler Bailly Consulting, Diagnostics of the Candidate Energos for the Commercialization Program, July 1997
9. Russian Power Sector Review, World Bank, Issue dated January 20, 1998
10. Latinina, Yulia, Don't Get into It- You'll Get Killed! in Izvestia May 13,1998
11. Hagler Bailly Team in Armenia, Application of Promissory Notes in the Russian Power Sector, May 1998
12. Annual Reports of RAO UES for 1996 and 1997
13. International Company for Finance and Investments, Moscow, Russian Utilities, Occasional Review, August 1997
14. Bank Paribas, International Equity Research Paper on Mosenergo, May 1998
15. EBRD President's Report on Corporate Loan to AO Mosenergo, November 1997
16. Russia: Barter Transactions, March 4, 1998 Update communicated by Jonathan Walters
17. Correspondence among Bank staff on Russian Power Sector 1997-98
18 Action Program to Improve Efficiency and to Further Reforms in the Russian Power Sector- RAO UES Document 1998
19. Energy Report on the Russian Territories of the Barents Region, Barents Group Oy, Finland, September 1997
20. The Russian Power Sector- A Long Struggle to Growth, CAIB Investment Bank AG, September 1998
21. Summary of the proceedings of the Collections Conference for AO Energos organized by RAO UES in October 1998- by Igor S. Sorokin, November 1998
22 Russian Utilities- Morgan Stanley Dean Witter Emerging Markets Investments Research dated February 26, 1998

PRIVATIZATION IN KAZAKHSTAN

Kazakhstan has an installed power generating capacity of about 17800 MW. About 75% of this is coal fired thermal power stations (GRES), a small portion of the remaining capacity is oil or gas fired and the rest are mostly hydro power stations (GES) . About 30% of the total capacity is in the form of Combined Heat and Power plants. With the collapse of communism and disintegration of Soviet Union, Kazakhstan power sector deteriorated considerably. Collections reached a very low level and cash collections formed a very small part of collections. Owing to inadequate funds, the power system could not be maintained, and only 13000 MW of generating capacity was believed to be in a condition suitable for operation. Power stations could not buy fuel for want of money and the country faced extensive power shortages despite having surplus capacity.

A Presidential Decree was issued in 1995 unbundling the hitherto vertically integrated utility and establishing a Russian model based two tier hierarchical system. The National Electric Company owned the transmission grid and the National dispatch system as well as the larger generating units of national significance. The regional distribution companies (energos) retained ownership of the remaining generating units of regional significance and the distribution systems. The National Company handled imports and exports of power and also the inter-regional trade in power. The generating units could also sell power directly to certain customers assigned to them. The chronic insolvency of the National Electric Company dealt a blow to this arrangement and further restructuring of the power sector took place.

Thus in 1996 about 82% of the total generating capacity--covering 37 generating plants-- was privatized. Currently about 90% of the capacity is privatized.[66] Of these only six units in Altaienergo were placed under a 20 year Management contract with AES-Silk Road. A new government owned company under the name KEGOC was set up in July 1997 to own the transmission grid and handle load dispatch and this company was asked to manage the remaining generating units under a management contract. Energos were left with distribution responsibility only and there are 18 such Energos. Three of these (Alamatyenergo, Karagandaenergo, Kokshetauenergo) were privatized in 1996. Ten energos have been placed under the management of KEGOC and the remaining 5 are being directly supervised by the State Privatization Committee. Tractebel S.A., purchased not only the Almatyenergo, but also the generating facilities, the CHP plants and the district heat distribution systems there.

The Anti-Monopolies Committee (AMC) acts as the regulator for the energy sector. It sets ceiling prices for the generating units for sale of electricity to the wholesale market, based on cost-plus considerations. The generating units can also directly contract with distribution companies and large consumers. Due to lack of demand, inability of distribution companies to pay and surplus generating capacity, actual prices charged for generated electricity had been much lower than the ceiling prices notified by AMC. Transmission and distribution tariffs are also set by AMC and are revised every quarter based on allowable costs. Transmission tariff consists of a fixed charge expressed as

---

[66] Most of the generating stations appear to have been sold at throw away prices.

Tenge / kWh and a distance charge expressed as Tenge / kWh / km. Retail tariff for the distribution is heavily influenced by central and local political interference, and the distribution margin had been kept deliberately low disallowing a number of legitimate costs, resulting in the financial unviability of the distribution entities. Distribution margin at US cents 0.9 / kWh is estimated to be 22% lower than the actual costs in 1997.

In respect of the 10 distribution companies under the management of KEGOC, collections improved to 93% in 1997 due to measures including: (1) prepayment requirements; and (2) aggressive disconnection of non-payers and occasionally even the distribution company (energo) from the HV grid. KEGOC's own collection for transmission services is about 72%--better than in previous years. Of the 10 distribution companies with KEGOC, three had collections of 70% only. In any case overall cash collection was only 33% of the sales. The remaining 60% was in the form of barters and set-off. In distribution companies with mostly agricultural consumers, cash collection was only 13-15% of sales. Generation companies have a collection performance even less favorable. The outstanding debts of distribution companies under KEGOC is believed to be of the order of $500 million including wage arrears of 2 months. Flexibility in valuing barter transactions makes the balance sheets of these companies suspect, severely eroding their ability to raise finance in the capital markets.

The retail tariff varies widely among the various distribution companies in the country. The average tariff for Kazakhstan as a whole has been estimated to be about US cents 4.4 / kWh in June 1998. This consists of generation cost of 2.0 cents, transmission costs of 0.5 cents, distribution margin of 0.9 cent and cost of T&D losses of 1.0 cent. Household tariffs were 10 to 15% lower than the industrial tariffs.

The experience of Tractebel S.A., in this milieu, is unique and noteworthy. It purchased not only the power distribution franchise in the Almatyenergo, but also acquired the related generation facilities (about 830 MW), CHP units, and the district heating distribution system at highly attractive prices. At the time of the acquisition, the power tariff was US cents 2.0/kWh and cash collections were at a low of 30%. The company had large wage arrears and no cash to buy fuel. Tractebel injected working capital, improved the generation and distribution facilities and achieved dramatically improved collection performance. Its collections reached 90% for power and 85% for district heating. Tariffs were raised to US cents 5/kWh through its efforts. The percentage of cash collections improved equally dramatically. This was achieved by the pursuit of aggressive and relentless disconnection policy towards defaulting consumers, including high profile ones such as the ministries of government, the military establishments and the like. This had an excellent demonstration effect resulting in every one getting into the discipline of paying their dues on time and paying it in cash. In most places it is normally difficult to deal with non-payers for the heat bill, as it is unpractical to disconnect heat consumers. Since Tractebel was doing both power and heat distribution, it sent one bill for both, and disconnected *power supply* when the customer defaulted in *heat* payment. It also devised creative solutions to the problem of privileged consumers. It has a healthy cash flow and no wage arrears problem and has put through a comprehensive rehabilitation and investment program and is also planning to convert the CHP plants for natural gas firing, when gas supply becomes assured.

The experience of AES- Silk Road, a subsidiary of AES of USA, in Kazakhstan is also somewhat similar. It acquired Ekibastuz I power station consisting of eight 500 MW supercritical coal fired thermal power plants built during 1980-85 at a price of US $ 5.0 million, restored and operated two units. In the course of two years, its collections have reached 90% consisting of 35% cash, 40% of cash equivalents or immediately cashable barter, and 15% of long term barter. It has no wage arrears and has a positive cash flow. It was achieved by a simple and consistent refusal to supply free power. This company also later acquired the power and heat facilities of Altaienergo (over 1400 MW for power and 2000 MW for heat) at about US $ 22.0 million. Here too they had to discipline their industrial consumers, overcome Mafia- like owners of heat network and achieved a high level of collections by pursuing a strict policy of disconnecting defaulting customers. They filed cases against defaulting Energos for bankruptcy and in some instances acquired the defaulting heat networks to improve collections. Wage arrears were cleared by paying the arrears in 12 installments and systems were working well. Last winter the city of Ust Kamenogorsk, close to Siberia, was considered the warmest in all Kazakhstan! The company is also making capital investments to complete the ongoing Shulbinsk Hydro project.

The imaginative **method used by this company to collect arrears from defaulting heat consumers is worthy of note.** While it was not possible to disconnect individual apartments for payment default, they devised methods to disconnect heat supply to the entire apartment block. The paying apartments inconvenienced by such disconnection were pacified by giving them electric space heaters free of charge and paying their incremental electricity bills. Heat supply to the apartment block was not resumed till all the apartments settled their dues. Meanwhile, as a humanitarian gesture, the public shelter (community hall) in the town was heated free of charge and the occupants of non-paying apartments without heat supply were informed that they could spend the nights in the public shelter to escape the discomfort of intense cold. When everyone settled his dues, and heat supply was resumed, the electric space heaters were withdrawn for reuse in other similar apartment blocks. By a strict adherence to such a routine, the company was able to discourage defaults and improve collection performance.

The experience of these two cases show how determined corporate governance can dramatically improve performance. They also indicate the efficacy of the policy of refusing to supply free power and disconnection of service to defaulting customers. They highlight the effectiveness of strategic privatization to qualified investors. The experience of Tractebel proves that that the combination of heat and power distribution in one company may help in overcoming the otherwise intractable problem of heat arrears. It may not however be easily replicated everywhere.

REFERENCES

1. BTOR of Bank mission Dated 29 June 1998
2. Electric Power and Telecom in Kazakhstan- a paper by R. E. Anderson dated 6 March 1998
3. Presentation by Jim Ellison of AES- Silk Road in Ukraine Cash Collection Conference of USAID in May 1998

Distributors of World Bank Group Publications

Prices and credit terms vary from country to country. Consult your local distributor before placing an order.

ARGENTINA
World Publications SA
Av. Cordoba 1877
1120 Ciudad de Buenos Aires
Tel: (54 11) 4815-8156
Fax: (54 11) 4815-8156
E-mail: wpbooks@infovia.com.ar

AUSTRALIA, FIJI, PAPUA NEW GUINEA, SOLOMON ISLANDS, VANUATU, AND SAMOA
D.A. Information Services
648 Whitehorse Road
Mitcham 3132, Victoria
Tel: (61) 3 9210 7777
Fax: (61) 3 9210 7788
E-mail: service@dadirect.com.au
URL: http://www.dadirect.com.au

AUSTRIA
Gerold and Co.
Weihburggasse 26
A-1011 Wien
Tel: (43 1) 512-47-31-0
Fax: (43 1) 512-47-31-29
URL: http://www.gerold.co/at.online

BANGLADESH
Micro Industries Development
Assistance Society (MIDAS)
House 5, Road 16
Dhanmondi R/Area
Dhaka 1209
Tel: (880 2) 326427
Fax: (880 2) 811188

BELGIUM
Jean De Lannoy
Av. du Roi 202
1060 Brussels
Tel: (32 2) 538-5169
Fax: (32 2) 538-0841

BRAZIL
Publicacões Tecnicas Internacionais
Ltda.
Rua Peixoto Gomide, 209
01409 Sao Paulo, SP.
Tel: (55 11) 259-6644
Fax: (55 11) 258-6990
E-mail: postmaster@pti.uol.br
URL: http://www.uol.br

CANADA
Renouf Publishing Co. Ltd.
5369 Canotek Road
Ottawa, Ontario K1J 9J3
Tel: (613) 745-2665
Fax: (613) 745-7660
E-mail:
order.dept@renoufbooks.com
URL: http:// www.renoufbooks.com

CHINA
China Financial & Economic
Publishing House
8, Da Fo Si Dong Jie
Beijing
Tel: (86 10) 6401-7365
Fax: (86 10) 6401-7365

China Book Import Centre
P.O. Box 2825
Beijing

Chinese Corporation for Promotion
of Humanities
52, You Fang Hu Tong,
Xuan Nei Da Jie
Beijing
Tel: (86 10) 660 72 494
Fax: (86 10) 660 72 494

COLOMBIA
Infoenlace Ltda.
Carrera 6 No. 51-21
Apartado Aereo 34270
Santafé de Bogotá, D.C.
Tel: (57 1) 285-2798
Fax: (57 1) 285-2798

COTE D'IVOIRE
Center d'Edition et de Diffusion
Africaines (CEDA)
04 B.P. 541
Abidjan 04
Tel: (225) 24 6510; 24 6511
Fax: (225) 25 0567

CYPRUS
Center for Applied Research
Cyprus College
6, Diogenes Street, Engomi
P.O. Box 2006
Nicosia
Tel: (357 2) 59-0730
Fax: (357 2) 66-2051

CZECH REPUBLIC
USIS, NIS Prodejna
Havelkova 22
130 00 Prague 3
Tel: (420 2) 2423 1486
Fax: (420 2) 2423 1114
URL: http://www.nis.cz/

DENMARK
SamfundsLitteratur
Rosenoerns Allé 11
DK-1970 Frederiksberg C
Tel: (45 35) 351942
Fax: (45 35) 357822
URL: http://www.sl.cbs.dk

ECUADOR
Libri Mundi
Libreria Internacional
P.O. Box 17-01-3029
Juan Leon Mera 851
Quito
Tel: (593 2) 521-606; (593 2) 544-185
Fax: (593 2) 504-209
E-mail: librimu1@librimundi.com.ec
E-mail: librimu2@librimundi.com.ec

CODEU
Ruiz de Castilla 763, Edif. Expocolor
Primer piso, Of. #2
Quito
Tel/Fax: (593 2) 507-383; 253-091
E-mail: codeu@impsat.net.ec

EGYPT, ARAB REPUBLIC OF
Al Ahram Distribution Agency
Al Galaa Street
Cairo
Tel: (20 2) 578-6083
Fax: (20 2) 578-6833

The Middle East Observer
41, Sherif Street
Cairo
Tel: (20 2) 393-9732
Fax: (20 2) 393-9732

FINLAND
Akateeminen Kirjakauppa
P.O. Box 128
FIN-00101 Helsinki
Tel: (358 0) 121 4418
Fax: (358 0) 121-4435
E-mail: akatilaus@stockmann.fi
URL: http://www.akateeminen.com

FRANCE
Editions Eska; DBJ
48, rue Gay Lussac
75005 Paris
Tel: (33-1) 55-42-73-08
Fax: (33-1) 43-29-91-67

GERMANY
UNO-Verlag
Poppelsdorfer Allee 55
53115 Bonn
Tel: (49 228) 949020
Fax: (49 228) 217492
URL: http://www.uno-verlag.de
E-mail: unoverlag@aol.com

GHANA
Epp Books Services
P.O. Box 44
TUC
Accra
Tel: 223 21 778843
Fax: 223 21 779099

GREECE
Papasotiriou S.A.
35, Stournara Str.
106 82 Athens
Tel: (30 1) 364-1826
Fax: (30 1) 364-8254

HAITI
Culture Diffusion
5, Rue Capois
C.P. 257
Port-au-Prince
Tel: (509) 23 9260
Fax: (509) 23 4858

HONG KONG, CHINA; MACAO
Asia 2000 Ltd.
Sales & Circulation Department
302 Seabird House
22-28 Wyndham Street, Central
Hong Kong, China
Tel: (852) 2530-1409
Fax: (852) 2526-1107
E-mail: sales@asia2000.com.hk
URL: http://www.asia2000.com.hk

HUNGARY
Euro Info Service
Margitszgeti Europa Haz
H-1138 Budapest
Tel: (36 1) 350 80 24, 350 80 25
Fax: (36 1) 350 90 32
E-mail: euroinfo@mail.matav.hu

INDIA
Allied Publishers Ltd.
751 Mount Road
Madras - 600 002
Tel: (91 44) 852-3938
Fax: (91 44) 852-0649

INDONESIA
Pt. Indira Limited
Jalan Borobudur 20
P.O. Box 181
Jakarta 10320
Tel: (62 21) 390-4290
Fax: (62 21) 390-4289

IRAN
Ketab Sara Co. Publishers
Khaled Eslamboli Ave., 6th Street
Delafrooz Alley No. 8
P.O. Box 15745-733
Tehran 15117
Tel: (98 21) 8717819; 8716104
Fax: (98 21) 8712479
E-mail: ketab-sara@neda.net.ir

Kowkab Publishers
P.O. Box 19575-511
Tehran
Tel: (98 21) 258-3723
Fax: (98 21) 258-3723

IRELAND
Government Supplies Agency
Oifig an tSoláthair
4-5 Harcourt Road
Dublin 2
Tel: (353 1) 661-3111
Fax: (353 1) 475-2670

ISRAEL
Yozmot Literature Ltd.
P.O. Box 56055
3 Yohanan Hasandlar Street
Tel Aviv 61560
Tel: (972 3) 5285-397
Fax: (972 3) 5285-397

R.O.Y. International
PO Box 13056
Tel Aviv 61130
Tel: (972 3) 649 9469
Fax: (972 3) 648 6039
E-mail: royil@netvision.net.il
URL: http://www.royint.co.il

Palestinian Authority/Middle East
Index Information Services
P.O.B. 19502 Jerusalem
Tel: (972 2) 6271219
Fax: (972 2) 6271634

ITALY, LIBERIA
Licosa Commissionaria Sansoni SPA
Via Duca Di Calabria, 1/1
Casella Postale 552
50125 Firenze
Tel: (39 55) 645-415
Fax: (39 55) 641-257
E-mail: licosa@ftbcc.it
URL: http://www.ftbcc.it/licosa

JAMAICA
Ian Randle Publishers Ltd.
206 Old Hope Road, Kingston 6
Tel: 876-927-2085
Fax: 876-977-0243
E-mail: irpl@colis.com

JAPAN
Eastern Book Service
3-13 Hongo 3-chome, Bunkyo-ku
Tokyo 113
Tel: (81 3) 3818-0861
Fax: (81 3) 3818-0864
E-mail: orders@svt-ebs.co.jp
URL:
http://www.bekkoame.or.jp/~svt-ebs

KENYA
Africa Book Service (E.A.) Ltd.
Quaran House, Mfangano Street
P.O. Box 45245
Nairobi
Tel: (254 2) 223 641
Fax: (254 2) 330 272

Legacy Books
Loita House
Mezzanine 1
P.O. Box 68077
Nairobi
Tel: (254) 2-330853, 221426
Fax: (254) 2-330854, 561654
E-mail: Legacy@form-net.com

KOREA, REPUBLIC OF
Dayang Books Trading Co.
International Division
783-20, Pangba Bon-Dong,
Socho-ku
Seoul
Tel: (82 2) 536-9555
Fax: (82 2) 536-0025
E-mail: seamap@chollian.net

Eulyoo Publishing Co., Ltd.
46-1, Susong-Dong
Jongro-Gu
Seoul
Tel: (82 2) 734-3515
Fax: (82 2) 732-9154

LEBANON
Librairie du Liban
P.O. Box 11-9232
Beirut
Tel: (961 9) 217 944
Fax: (961 9) 217 434
E-mail: hsayegh@librairie-du-liban.com.lb
URL: http://www.librairie-du-liban.com.lb

MALAYSIA
University of Malaya Cooperative
Bookshop, Limited
P.O. Box 1127
Jalan Pantai Baru
59700 Kuala Lumpur
Tel: (60 3) 756-5000
Fax: (60 3) 755-4424
E-mail: umkoop@tm.net.my

MEXICO
INFOTEC
Av. San Fernando No. 37
Col. Toriello Guerra
14050 Mexico, D.F.
Tel: (52 5) 624-2800
Fax: (52 5) 624-2822
E-mail: infotec@rtn.net.mx
URL: http://rtn.net.mx

Mundi-Prensa Mexico S.A. de C.V.
c/Rio Panuco, 141-Colonia
Cuauhtemoc
06500 Mexico, D.F.
Tel: (52 5) 533-5658
Fax: (52 5) 514-6799

NEPAL
Everest Media International Services
(P.) Ltd.
GPO Box 5443
Kathmandu
Tel: (977 1) 416 026
Fax: (977 1) 224 431

NETHERLANDS
De Lindeboom/Internationale
Publicaties b.v.-
P.O. Box 202, 7480 AE Haaksbergen
Tel: (31 53) 574-0004
Fax: (31 53) 572-9296
E-mail: lindeboo@worldonline.nl
URL: http://www.worldonline.nl/~lindeboo

NEW ZEALAND
EBSCO NZ Ltd.
Private Mail Bag 99914
New Market
Auckland
Tel: (64 9) 524-8119
Fax: (64 9) 524-8067

Oasis Official
P.O. Box 3627
Wellington
Tel: (64 4) 499 1551
Fax: (64 4) 499 1972
E-mail: oasis@actrix.gen.nz
URL: http://www.oasisbooks.co.nz/

NIGERIA
University Press Limited
Three Crowns Building Jericho
Private Mail Bag 5095
Ibadan
Tel: (234 22) 41-1356
Fax: (234 22) 41-2056

PAKISTAN
Mirza Book Agency
65, Shahrah-e-Quaid-e-Azam
Lahore 54000
Tel: (92 42) 735 3601
Fax: (92 42) 576 3714

Oxford University Press
5 Bangalore Town
Sharae Faisal
PO Box 13033
Karachi-75350
Tel: (92 21) 446307
Fax: (92 21) 4547640
E-mail: ouppak@TheOffice.net

Pak Book Corporation
Aziz Chambers 21, Queen's Road
Lahore
Tel: (92 42) 636 3222; 636 0885
Fax: (92 42) 636 2328
E-mail: pbc@brain.net.pk

PERU
Editorial Desarrollo SA
Apartado 3824, Ica 242 OF. 106
Lima 1
Tel: (51 14) 285380
Fax: (51 14) 286628

PHILIPPINES
International Booksource Center Inc.
1127-A Antipolo St, Barangay,
Venezuela
Makati City
Tel: (63 2) 896 6501; 6505; 6507
Fax: (63 2) 896 1741

POLAND
International Publishing Service
Ul. Piekna 31/37
00-677 Warzawa
Tel: (48 2) 628-6089
Fax: (48 2) 621-7255
E-mail: books%ips@ikp.atm.com.pl
URL:
http://www.ipscg.waw.pl/ips/export

PORTUGAL
Livraria Portugal
Apartado 2681, Rua Do Carm
o 70-74
1200 Lisbon
Tel: (1) 347-4982
Fax: (1) 347-0264

ROMANIA
Compani De Librarii Bucuresti S.A.
Str. Lipscani no. 26, sector 3
Bucharest
Tel: (40 1) 313 9645
Fax: (40 1) 312 4000

RUSSIAN FEDERATION
Isdatelstvo <Ves Mir>
9a, Kolpachniy Pereulok
Moscow 101831
Tel: (7 095) 917 87 49
Fax: (7 095) 917 92 59
ozimarin@glasnet.ru

**SINGAPORE; TAIWAN, CHINA
MYANMAR; BRUNEI**
Hemisphere Publication Services
41 Kallang Pudding Road #04-03
Golden Wheel Building
Singapore 349316
Tel: (65) 741-5166
Fax: (65) 742-9356
E-mail: ashgate@asianconnect.com

SLOVENIA
Gospodarski vestnik Publishing
Group
Dunajska cesta 5
1000 Ljubljana
Tel: (386 61) 133 83 47; 132 12 30
Fax: (386 61) 133 80 30
E-mail: repansekj@gvestnik.si

SOUTH AFRICA, BOTSWANA
For single titles:
Oxford University Press Southern
Africa
Vasco Boulevard, Goodwood
P.O. Box 12119, N1 City 7463
Cape Town
Tel: (27 21) 595 4400
Fax: (27 21) 595 4430
E-mail: oxford@oup.co.za

For subscription orders:
International Subscription Service
P.O. Box 41095
Craighall
Johannesburg 2024
Tel: (27 11) 880-1448
Fax: (27 11) 880-6248
E-mail: iss@is.co.za

SPAIN
Mundi-Prensa Libros, S.A.
Castello 37
28001 Madrid
Tel: (34 91) 4 363700
Fax: (34 91) 5 753998
E-mail: libreria@mundiprensa.es
URL: http://www.mundiprensa.com/

Mundi-Prensa Barcelona
Consell de Cent, 391
08009 Barcelona
Tel: (34 3) 488-3492
Fax: (34 3) 487-7659
E-mail: barcelona@mundiprensa.es

SRI LANKA, THE MALDIVES
Lake House Bookshop
100, Sir Chittampalam Gardiner
Mawatha
Colombo 2
Tel: (94 1) 32105
Fax: (94 1) 432104
E-mail: LHL@sri.lanka.net

SWEDEN
Wennergren-Williams AB
P. O. Box 1305
S-171 25 Solna
Tel: (46 8) 705-97-50
Fax: (46 8) 27-00-71
E-mail: mail@wwi.se

SWITZERLAND
Librairie Payot Service Institutionnel
C(tm)tes-de-Montbenon 30
1002 Lausanne
Tel: (41 21) 341-3229
Fax: (41 21) 341-3235

ADECO Van Diermen
EditionsTechniques
Ch. de Lacuez 41
CH1807 Blonay
Tel: (41 21) 943 2673
Fax: (41 21) 943 3605

THAILAND
Central Books Distribution
306 Silom Road
Bangkok 10500
Tel: (66 2) 2336930-9
Fax: (66 2) 237-8321

**TRINIDAD & TOBAGO
AND THE CARRIBBEAN**
Systematics Studies Ltd.
St. Augustine Shopping Center
Eastern Main Road, St. Augustine
Trinidad & Tobago, West Indies
Tel: (868) 645-8466
Fax: (868) 645-8467
E-mail: tobe@trinidad.net

UGANDA
Gustro Ltd.
PO Box 9997, Madhvani Building
Plot 16/4 Jinja Rd.
Kampala
Tel: (256 41) 251 467
Fax: (256 41) 251 468
E-mail: gus@swiftuganda.com

UNITED KINGDOM
Microinfo Ltd.
P.O. Box 3, Omega Park, Alton,
Hampshire GU34 2PG
England
Tel: (44 1420) 86848
Fax: (44 1420) 89889
E-mail: wbank@microinfo.co.uk
URL: http://www.microinfo.co.uk

The Stationery Office
51 Nine Elms Lane
London SW8 5DR
Tel: (44 171) 873-8400
Fax: (44 171) 873-8242
URL: http://www.the-stationery-office.co.uk/

VENEZUELA
Tecni-Ciencia Libros, S.A.
Centro Cuidad Comercial Tamanco
Nivel C2, Caracas
Tel: (58 2) 959 5547; 5035; 0016
Fax: (58 2) 959 5636

ZAMBIA
University Bookshop, University of
Zambia
Great East Road Campus
P.O. Box 32379
Lusaka
Tel: (260 1) 252 576
Fax: (260 1) 253 952

ZIMBABWE
Academic and Baobab Books (Pvt.)
Ltd.
4 Conald Road, Graniteside
P.O. Box 567
Harare
Tel: 263 4 755035
Fax: 263 4 781913